ALL BURGOS
and province

Text: Carlos de Haro

Photographs: Julián Sáez de María, Mario Sarrià and
FISA-Escudo de Oro Photographic Archives.

Design, lay-out and printing completely created
by the technical department of
EDITORIAL FISA ESCUDO DE ORO S.A.

ESCUDO DE ORO

View of Burgos from the viewpoint of the castle.

INTRODUCTION

Located in the North of the Community of Castile and Leon, the province of Burgos is rich in landscapes and history. In a natural environment of 14,300 km², marked out by proud mountains, powerful rivers, splendid valleys and captivating plains, man comes leaving his mark, as the prehistoric sites of Ojo Guareña or Atapuerca testify, from remote times. Through these lands of short, cold winters and hot summers, came Cantabrians, Autrigones, Turmodigos, Arevacos and Vacceos. Later Romans, Goths and Arabs would arrive. These last comers sowed the territory with uncertainties, provoking the flight of the population towards the mountains in the North.

With the first Christian victories, the plains and valleys of the province began to recuperate their inhabitants. It was then when Alfonso III, king of Leon, ordered Count Diego Rodríguez Porcelos to found a walled city on the banks of the river Arlanzón in order to halt the advance of the Saracens. It was around the year 884 when Burgos was born. It wasn't long before the city became an important stronghold of the young Castile. Names like that of Fernán González, the first independent count of Castile, or that of El Cid Campeador, who was feared and respected by the Arabs and Christians alike, contributed to exalt the history of Burgos.

The transfer of the Episcopal seat from Oca to Burgos in 1075 marked a historic milestone for the city and the nearby towns, since it brought about the construction of temples, monasteries and hospitals in a short time. The passage of pilgrims, who crossed the province following the Way of Saint James, were also decisive in the economic development of these lands. Centuries later, the exportation of wool to the most important European markets constituted the main source of wealth in Burgos. At the end of the 15th

2

Way of Saint James: chapel of San Amaro, outside of Burgos, and bridge of Malatos, in the Park of the Island.

Palace of the Audience or Justice, constructed at the end of the 19th century.

century, the Catholic Kings conceded the monopoly of said trade to the city, which would be regulated by the so-called Consulate of Burgos. At the same time, the University of Merchants was founded. This period of splendor lasted until the second half of the 16th century. During these years, large, majestic palaces were erected and buildings and streets were renovated. However, right before the century's end, the first symptoms of decadence were observed. The loss of political and economic power, to the benefit of Madrid, and two plagues, occurring in 1565 and 1599, led Burgos and its province to a gradual decline that would become more evident in the 17th century.

Palace of Deputies: allegorical painting of El Cid Campeador, work of Vela Zanetti. Photo ceded by the Provincial Legislature of Burgos. Herraiz photographs.

After some unsuccessful initiatives carried out in the 18th century, such as the attempt to restore the Consulate for continuing the wool trade, the 19th century would bring diverse changes to Burgos that would entail its recuperation. One of these was the constitution of the provinces in 1834 and the consequential creation of the Provincial Council, which would have its seat in the city, as well as the Territorial Audience, the Military Headquarters and the Archbishopric. To strengthen this administrative reordering, a profound reform was produced, which would culminate with the construction of various public buildings, the avenue Paseo del Espolón, the park Parque de la Isla or the district of Santa Clara. The improvement of connections in the entire province and the consolidation of an incipient fabric industry were factors that marked the first decades of the 20th century and that laid the bases of present-day Burgos. Currently, the province has about 362,000 inhabitants, 166,000 of whom live in the capital.

Archbishop's Palace, construction dated in 1916.

The avenue Paseo del Espolón, the most emblematic of the city, stretches from the plaza of Mío Cid up to the Arch of Santa María, in the background of the image.

Plaza of Castile. Artistic "vase" work by local artist Fortunato Julián.

The Park Parque de la Isla is an extensive orchard dotted with monumental remains like the so-called Arches of Castilfalé (upper image) and the Roman doorway (12th century) of the church Nuestra Señora de la Llana of Cerezo de Río Tirón (lower image).

Burgos is a city that lives looking toward the future while not renouncing its cultural legacy that its fertile history has left it. For that reason, it revels in its stone monuments, protecting it from the aggression that is sometimes produced in the name of urbanism. It is also a city with long and tranquil avenues, with areas especially designed for this need. The spacious avenue **Paseo del Espolón**, along the banks of the Arlanzón, is the busiest of them all. In summer, it is populated by sidewalk cafés that invite chatting and tranquility. Another delicious place is the park **Parque de la Isla**, which begins at the plaza of Castile. In it, a great diversity of trees, a pleasant pool and some artwork, like the Arches of Castilfalé or the Roman façade of the temple Cerezo de Río Tirón. The garden **Jardín del Empecinado**, the **Paseo de la Quinta** or the **Parque del Cerro del Castillo** serve as reminder of the respect that this city feels for the natural setting.

Honoring the heroes, who in some way appear tied to its history, is another of the characteristics that defines Burgos. The street **Fernán González** houses the monument dedicated to this noble, also known as the "Good Count", which stands where it is believed his house was. It has the form of an arch and dates back to 1586. A few meters away, there is the **funerary monument of Empecinado**, the popular warrior who harassed the Napoleanic troops with shrewdness and few means during the War of Independence. And next to the Gate of San Martín, stands the so-called **Solar del Cid**; a simple monument from 1784 located on the terrain that the residence of Rodrigo Díaz de Vivar occupied.

The evocation of the figure of El Cid doesn't end here. In the **plaza del Mío Cid,** you can see a majestic equestrian statue of the Burgos hero, carved in 1955, on the back of his inseparable Babieca. Opposite, on both sides of the bridge of San Pablo, appear eight personalities related to El Cid, among them, his wife Doña Jimena and his son Diego.

But Burgos is also the ringing its church bells, the echo of the steps of thousands of pilgrims that crossed on the province's stretch of the Way of Saint James, the light babble of the crystalline waters of the Arlanzón and, above all, its people, who after all are the true protagonists of all the stories that the city tells us.

Funerary monument of the Empecinado.

Solar del Cid.

Bridge of San Pablo.

9

Cathedral of Burgos. Gate of Sarmental.

Nocturnal view of the Cathedral. ▷

THE CATHEDRAL

Declared by UNESCO in 1984 a World Heritage Site, the Cathedral of Burgos is, apart from the most emblematic monument of the city, an authentic marvel of Spanish Gothic art. The harmony of its lines, the intense and moving labor with which its stone was carved and even its location, on that gentle hillside that overlooks the banks of the Arlanzón, give the temple an image of power and singular beauty. It started to be built in 1221 by initiative of the bishop Mauricio and the king of Castile and Leon, Fernando III the Saint, over the ancient Roman church that another monarch, Alfonso VI, had ordered erected at

the end of the 11th century. Despite that the majority of the works were done during the 13th century and that its consecration dates back to 1260, it would have to wait until the second half of the 18th century when it was totally finished.

Little is known about the identities of the first masters who directed the project, although it is believed that they came from France, due to the presence of some typical Gothic elements from that country in the Burgos cathedral. Later, in the 15th century, artists of German origin took over. The characteristic needles that crown the towers of the main façade are due to them and Juan de Colonia, in particular. The dome, also a work of his, was knocked down in 1539,

Dome of the Cathedral. Photo: Enrique del Rivero.

Main façade of the Cathedral. ▷

being replaced in the middle of the 16th century by the splendid construction that we now see, work of Juan de Vallejo.

The main entrance is situated in the beautiful plaza of Santa María. The façade, also known by this name, was remodeled first in 1663, the year the two side doors were transformed, and later in 1790, when the renovation of the central door was completed. The sides were then adorned with bas-relief of the Coronation and the Conception of the Virgin, while the center displayed a Greco-Roman façade accompanied by the figures of the kings Alfonso VI and Fernando III and the bishops Mauricio and Asterio. Two 13th-century towers, which flank the access, belong to an original work, upon which Juan de Colonia placed his celebrated octagonal-based, fretwork pinnacles. These

towers, as well as the dome and the finish of the chapel of Condestable, are an example of the slender lines and the taste for worked stone that characterize the so-called Flemish Gothic. On top of the doorway, a large rose window with a six-pointed star and, higher up, the so-called gallery of the kings, with eight sculptures of distinct Castillian monarchs and princes, stand out. These compositions, in which homage is rendered to the monarchic institution, are very typical of French cathedrals. In this case, the artists were inspired by the cathedral of Reims. Finishing off the complex is a vaulted niche with an image of the Virgin and the Christ child, with an inscription reading: "Pulcra es et decora" (You are pretty and beautiful).

The beautiful Gothic door of the Sarmental, in the

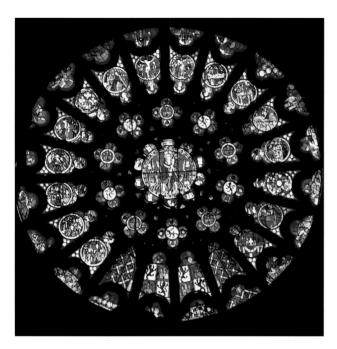

Rose window of Sarmental.

Coronería door.

plaza of Rey San Fernando, allows access to the temple by one of the ends of the transept. It is dedicated to the magistracy of Christ, as can be appreciated in its magnificent tympanum. In it, the figure of Jesus showing the Book of Law and the evangelists writing at their desks appear. On the opposite side of the transept, the Coronería door, which is on the street Fernán González, is Gothic too. It was decorated with scenes of the Final Judgement. In this same part of the transept, although on the side facing the head of the cathedral, the door of the tannery was constructed at the beginning of the 16th century in plateresque style. Divided into three bodies, the center is represented by the martyrs of San Juan the Baptist and San Juan the Evangelist, and the upper part, an image of the Virgin, before whom the bishop Juan Rodríguez de Fonseca who is in charge of this door, prays.

Inside the cathedral, richly ornamented, has a Latin-cross floor and three spacious naves, transept, apse-aisle, and thirteen chapels. The total length of the temple measures 106 m and the transept is 59 m. The enormous pillars, upon which the grandiose structure rests, are cylindrical, with small, adjacent columns. One of the most curious elements of its decoration is the figure of the *Papamoscas* (Flycatcher), in the heights of the left nave. When the clock marks the time, this doll, whose origins might well date back to the 16th century, rings the bell when it opens its mouth.

Following the custom that is imposed upon the Spanish churches after the 16th century, the choir, originally placed at the head of the temple, occupies the central part of the central nave. The choir stalls, made throughout that century, allow a glimpse of the total expressive force of Renaissance art. The reclining statue of the bishop Mauricio, the founder of the cathedral, which was made in wood and covered with embossed copper in the middle of the 13th century, presides over this hall. On both sides of the choir stalls, there are two organs, one Baroque and the other Neoclassical.

Leaving the choir, right in the center of the transept, a sober, marble tombstone marks the grave of Rodrigo Díaz de Vivar, El Cid, and his wife, Doña Jimena.

During the second half of the 16th century, various artists, directed by the brothers Rodrigo and Martín de la Haya, participated in the composition of the magnificent and grandiose high altarpiece. Of Renaissance style, it is dedicated to Santa María the Elder, whose images presides over the complex. It

Central nave.

Left nave: the "Papamoscas".

consists of three horizontal bodies, a fourth as a crown and seven vertical strips decorated with figures of saints and apostles.

In the first chapel of the right nave, the Christ of Burgos, a beautiful image of the 16th century by an unknown artist, is venerated. It was brought over in 1836 from the monastery of San Agustín. With time, its popularity wouldn't only cross the boundaries of the province, but also those of Castile, and today, it is worshipped in Andalucía and in various countries of America, where it is known as the Lord of Burgos. Before arriving to the transept, we find the chapel of the Presentation, with an impressive tomb sculpted at the beginning of the 16th century in white alabaster of the canon Gonzalo Díez de Lerma; the chapel of the Reliquaries, which houses the Gothic images of

Choir stalls.

*High
altarpiece.*

Chapel of the Christ of Burgos.

Chapel of the Presentation.

the Virgin of Oca and the Virgin of the Miracle; and the chapel of San Juan de Sahagún, where the rococo-style altarpiece stands out.

Next to this last chapel, and already in the nave of the transept, the chapel of the Visitation is found, constructed in the middle of the 15th by Juan de Colonia. Of the diverse tombs that it contains, the one of greatest artistic value is that of the bishop Alonso de Cartagena, in the middle of the room. Facing the chapel, the doorway to the cloister, from the end of the 13th century, is located. In its tympanum, the baptism of Jesus is represented. Carved in the wood leaves of the door, at the close of the 15th century already, are the images of San Pedro and San Pablo, in the lower half, and the entrance of Jesus into Jerusalem and his departure from Limbo, in the upper half.

Passing the chapel of San Enrique, with a notable Ecce Homo, probably done at the end of the 15th century, the ante-sacristy is reached, through which the sacristy and the cloister is accessed. The sacristy was completely renovated between 1761 and 1765 following the Baroque tastes of the period. The cloister has not experienced any substantial modifications since it was constructed in the 13th century and today, it still preserves that atmosphere of peace and quiet and spirituality distinctive of the Gothic style of those years. With two floors, the upper one has numerous funerary monuments, the majority of which are destined to the burial of canons. The presence of pieces like the frontal and altarpiece of Mave (Palencia), whose origin dates back to the first half of the 13th century, also stands out.

Chapel of Lerma.

Chapel of San Juan de Sahagún.

In the rooms that connect the cloister, the Cathedral Museum is installed. So, the chapel of San Juan the Baptist, of the 14th century, houses pieces of gold work like communion cups, processional crosses or the reliquaries made at the end of the 15th century of San Pedro, San Pablo and Santiago. United to the afore mentioned since 1534, the chapel of Santiago is destined to painting and tapestries. In the chapel of Santa Catalina, which was the chapter house hall until 1596, there are sculptures, codexes (a Visigoth Bible from the 10th century among them) and diverse manuscripts, the most notable being the Letter of Arras from El Cid. In this chapel, from the beginning of the 14th century, we can contemplate its magnificent, starred vault, sustained upon eight arches of installment columns that come from some curious beams with naturalist repre-

sentations, and its polychrome doorway with the scene of the Descent of Christ from the Cross on the tympanum. The chapel of Corpus Christi also presents a suggestive doorway: on its tympanum, a Christ Judge surrounded by the figures of the Virgin, San Juan and four angels are distinguished. In the chapel, the Casket of El Cid that appears reflected in the famous poem of Cantar and a beautiful processional image of Christ tied to a column, carved in the 16th century by Diego de Siloé, are exhibited. Through this chapel, the Chapter house is accessed, containing the fascinating triptychs of the Adoration of the Kings or the Virgin with the Christ child. The cathedral archive is on the upper floor that conserves originals from the 10th century.

Already in the apse-aisle, five large reliefs of superb execution close what is the high chapel. They were done

*Cloister of the
Cathedral.*

21

Chapel of Santa Catalina.

The apse-aisle.

Chapel of the Condestable:
detail of high altarpiece.

between the end of the 15th century and the beginning of the 16th by the Frenchman Felipe de Vigarny. Facing these, the chapel of the Condestable, an octagonal-shaped area constructed by Simón de Colonia at the end of the 15th century, where Pedro Fernández de Velasco, the Condestable, and his wife, Mencía de Mendoza, are buried. Their reclining statues, situated in front of the central altarpiece and below a magnificent, starred vault, were carved in 1534 with extraordinary detail in Carrara marble by one of the numerous artists who participated in the decoration of the chapel, Felipe de Vigarny. By the same artist and by Diego de Siloé is the high altarpiece, which is dedicated to the Purification of the Virgin. The installment columns and the exquisite work done in stone proportion the chapel with an impressive sensation of weightlessness. Other

noteworthy elements are the banister of the entrance, from 1526, the Gothic tombs from the 16th century, where the bishops Pedro Rodríguez Quijada and Domingo Fernández Arroyuelo are buried, the altarpieces of Santa Ana and San Pedro and the different coats of arms of the family of the Condestable.

Also of Gothic style, but from the middle of the 13th century, is the chapel of San Gregorio. The tombs of the bishops Gonzalo de Hinojosa and Lope de Fontecha are its most valuable pieces. To the side, the chapel of the Annunciation conserves the gothic vault from the 13th century and a mannerist altarpiece done in 1540. The chapel of the Nativity, the last of the apse-aisle, is from the second half of the 16th century and its central altarpiece stands out, framed by a large arch, which is supported by both columns, and the lantern of the

Chapel of the Anunciation.

Chapel of the Nativity.

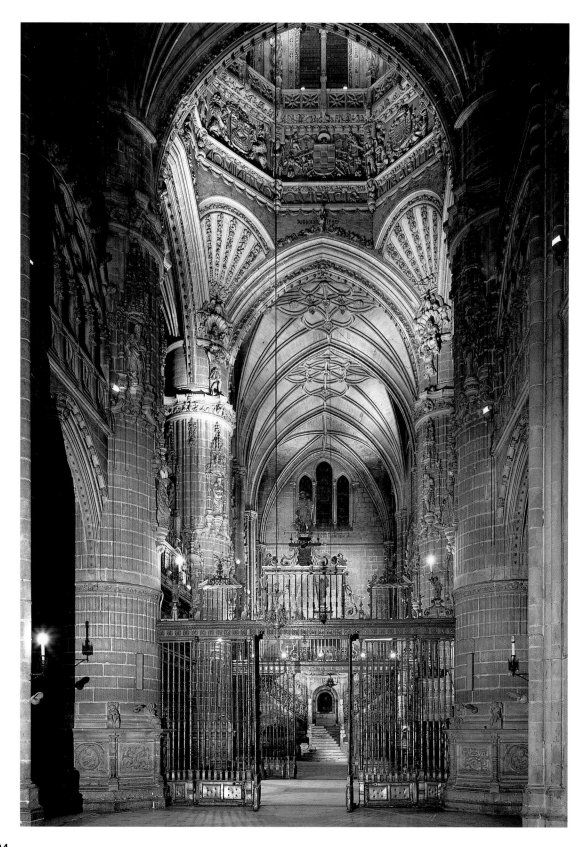

Nave of the transept.

Chapel of the Conception and Chapel of Santa Tecla.

cupola. Between this and the chapel of San Nicolas, the tomb of the humanist Pedro Fernández de Villegas, first translator of Dante in the Spanish language, is found. The chapel of San Nicolas is located in the transept. Dated at 1230, the late Roman style of the original can almost be identified already.

The end of the transept is crowned by the so-called Golden Staircase, built between 1519 and 1523 for allowing access from the Coronería door. Its artist, Diego de Siloé, was inspired by the models of the Italian Renaissance. The banister, filled with golden adornments, was designed a few years later by the French bars master Hilario.

The chapel of the Conception and Santa Ana completes the route through the cathedral, with a splendid high altarpiece that represents the genealogy of

Chapel of Santa Tecla: baptismal font.

the Virgin, and the chapel of Santa Tecla, built in the 18th century, as can be appreciated in its altarpiece, the Baroque canons. Inside, a baptismal font from the 13th century is kept.

CHURCH OF SAN NICOLAS

Situated to the left of the main façade of the Cathedral, is a Gothic temple from the beginning of the 15th century, constructed thanks to the donations of Gonzalo López Polanco, a prosperous Burgos merchant, of whom it is said even had a commercial house in Florence.

The simple façade, with a portico of elegant pointed arch presided over by the image of the title saint, contrasts with the richness inside. It is divided into three small naves, which are illuminated by two rose windows. In this sober, moving setting, the monumental high altarpiece, done by the workshop of Simón de Colonia at the beginning of the 16th century, stands out. At the margin of its beauty, this composition of rectangular tapestry form is noteworthy for having been done in stone, something that wasn't very common in Castile at the time. Divided into three vertical lanes, the two lateral ones house distinct biblical scenes, such as the images of saints and apostles. At the base of both, two Gothic tombs in which Gonzalo López Polanco, patrons of the temple, his brother and their respective wives are buried. The central lane, of greater width, is dominated by the sculpture of San Nicolas that Francisco de Colonia carved. Over this, a choir of angels surrounds the circle that represents the Coronation of the Virgin.

The Renaissance arch of the tomb of Fernando de Mena and María Sáenz de Oña and a Christ on the Cross, from the 15th century, are other elements of interest in this church.

PALACE OF MALUENDA OR OF CASTILFALÉ

Facing the Coronería door of the Cathedral, and in a site where the architect Simón de Colonia kept his residence, the Burgos noble Andrés de Maluenda erected this building in 1565 that today is the central office of the Municipal Archive. Occasional resi-

Palace of Castilfalé.

Church of San Esteban.

dence of Napoleon and Fernando VII, its last owner was the Count of Castilfalé, who, in 1969, ceded it to the government of the city.

A simple garden is the antechamber of this stone and brick construction, so characteristic of the urban landscape of Burgos. The artistic doorway, crowned by the Maluenda coat of arms, has a half-pointed arch framed by fine columns. Despite the successive renovations received, the last in 1985 with the aim of turning it into the Municipal Archive, the palace still preserves original elements. A beautiful covered stairway with a wooden coffered ceiling is the most significant.

CHURCH OF SAN ESTEBAN

Very close to the old castle of Burgos, this Gothic church is found. It was constructed to substitute an earlier Roman temple between the end of the 13th century and the first half of the 14th. Precisely, that proximity meant that on more than one occasion, it would receive some impact destined in principle to the castle. And so, in the 15th century already, the rose window, the towers and the pillars had to be rebuilt.

The doorway of San Esteban has certain similarities with that of the Coronería of the Cathedral. In both cases, the scene of the "Deesis" or Christ Judge, before whom the Virgin and San Juan intercede, appears on the tympanum. Here, though, the martyrdom of San Esteban was added to the lower part. Inside, three naves are distributed, with their respective apses, separated by large pilasters with small adjacent columns. The high choir, one of the temple's most interesting elements, was done by Simón de Colonia in the early years of the 16th century. Not any less valuable artistically are the Renaissance pulpit, from the same period, the cloister, which is accessed through a beautiful, Renaissance doorway or the various Gothic funerary complexes that are found in the side naves.

For a few years now, the church of San Esteban houses the **Museum of Altarpieces**, where altarpieces from distinct places of the province, basically from the 16th to 18th centuries, can be admired. Likewise, an interesting and cared-for selection of gold work pieces is displayed in the choir.

ARCH OF SAN ESTEBAN

During the last third of the 13th century, Alfonso X order the primitive wall that surrounded the castle expanded in order to extend the defenses of a city in constant expansion. The construction lasted until the 14th century, date of the Arch of San Esteban, surely the most interesting gate from an architectural perspective of all those that remain standing. Of Mudéjar style, it has a double horseshoe arch and two robust towers with square floors united by a gallery where six half-pointed arches open up. Built with masonry stone and brick, the Arch of San Esteban offers an image of extraordinary firmness that is reinforced by its defensive character.

THE CASTLE

On the mountain top that dominates the landscape of the city, the remains of the castle that gave Burgos its origins in the year 884 sticks out. At that time, it would play a determinant part in the wars that fol-

Arch of San Esteban.

View of Burgos from the viewpoint of the castle.

lowed the entrance of the Arabs into the Peninsula. At the end of the 15th century, it lived one of its most controversial historic passages. In the open conflict for the succession to the throne of Castile, the fort was placed at the service of the Beltraneja cause, while the city of Burgos supported the future queen Isabel the Catholic. Shortly after, it would be converted into an artillery park, although with time, it would have uses as diverse as a prison or occasional residence of illustrious guests. In 1736, a fire seriously damaged it. Restored by the Napoleanic army in 1808, these same troops would be the ones who, five years later, would dynamite it before retreating from the Burgos capital.

The recuperation work that began in 1992 has allowed the castle to receive part of its original aspect back. Some wall fragments, various towers, diverse galleries and a well, which is reached by going down a torturous stairwell of 300 steps, are visible. Archeological exploration on the mountain has also brought the

remains of a Roman church and three necropolises, belonging to distinct cultures, to light.

To its evident historical interest, the castle of Burgos adds the incentive of its privileged location. Today, spectacular images can be contemplated by going to its viewpoint.

ARCH OF SAN MARTÍN

Stone and brick were the materials used in the construction of this gate of the old wall through which the kings entered when visiting the city and the pilgrims left on their way to Santiago. From the 14th century, its Mudejar execution is manifested in the characteristic and beautiful horseshoe arch. Behind it, the main Jewish quarter of Burgos was found.

Very close by, in the avenue Paseo de los Cubos, the best conserved section of the wall that surrounded the perimeter of the population in the 13th century

Arch of San Martín.

can be appreciated. Its route, decided upon by the king Alfonso X himself, alternated straight walls with tower of semicircular front.

CHURCH OF SANTA ÁGUEDA

Tradition says, more than history, that it was in this church where El Cid Campeador made Alfonso VI swear that he hadn't participated in the death of his own brother, King Sancho II, assassinated at the gates of Zamora in 1072. The event, known as the swearing of Santa Gadea, helped the Leon monarch take possession of the throne of Castile, but it also helped obscure the relations between both in a definite way. Despite that, Alfonso VI would concede the hand of his cousin Doña Jimena to El Cid in 1074, with whom he had three children: two daughters, Cristina and

Church of Santa Águeda.

María, immortalized in the Cantar of Mío Cid as Doña Elvira and Doña Sol, and a boy called Diego.

The pilasters that sustain the only nave of this Roman temple, which would be witness to this event, barely remain, since the church dates from the 15th century and its head, from the 16th. Its simple entrance gives way to an interior characterized by its sobriety. Under its pronounced vaults, there are various Renaissance tombs of interest, like that of Diego Morisco and María de Toro. In the beautiful 16th century tomb of Alonso Delgadillo, the busts of San Pedro and San Pablo can be distinguished. Another noteworthy element is the chapel of the Escalada-Mendoza, built in the 16th century following Baroque tastes.

ARCH OF SANTA MARÍA

During the 16th century, some of the gates of the old medieval wall were partially or totally restored. Among those that experienced the greatest transformation is the Arch of Santa María, the most beautiful, well-known and original of them all. Its remodelation was entrusted to Juan Vallejo and Francisco de Colonia, who received the responsibility of erecting an arch of triumph in honor of the emperor Carlos V. The singular monument, concluded in 1553, appears flanked by two large circulars towers crowned by four small towers. In the central part, a series of niches contain the figures of distinct illustrious personalities of Castillian history. In the lower body,

Perspective of the Arch of Santa María with the Cathedral towers in the background.

Plaza of Mío Cid: Teatro Principal and equestrian statue of El Cid.

the statue of Count Diego Porcelos accompanied by the judges Laín Calvo and Nuño Rasura are distinguished in the upper part, Carlos V next to El Cid and Count Fernán González. Further up, the Guardian Angel of the city and two municipal mace-beares, and crowning the structure, Santa María, patron saint of Burgos.

Inside the arch, which was the seat of the Council of the locality until 1791, brings together some of the most representative elements of the city's history. The central room is presided over by a large mural, work of the Burgos painter Vela Zanetti, dedicated to Count Fernán González and it makes reference to the birth of Castile. In the so-called Hall of Poridad or the Secret, with an extraordinarily beautiful Mudejar coffered ceiling from the 14th century, pieces related to El Cid, like a reproduction of his famous sword Tiz. Also interesting is the **Museum of Pharmacy**, with objects related to this science from the 17th, 18th and 19th centuries.

TEATRO PRINCIPAL

After some doubts about where its best location would be, in 1843 a new municipal theater began to be built to substitute the old one on the street Puebla, which had become inadequate for the intense cultural life of Burgos at the time. The work, directed by the architect Francisco Angoitia, didn't develop easily either, since it was delayed several years due to a lack of funding. Finally, in 1858 the fabulous Teatro Principal (Main Theater), which came to enhance the emblematic and busy Paseo del Espolón, was inaugurated The building is a good example of the academic line predominant in the Spain of Isabel II, known as "Isabel style". The whole lower body, with its characteristic arches, was done in masonry stone, while on the upper floors, materials of lesser quality were used with the aim of meeting the budget. In 1884, a rotunda was added to the façade facing the Paseo del Espolón, where one of the recreational societies installed in the theater often organized their concerts. After many decades of abandonment that caused its deterioration, the theater was recuperated and opened its doors again on July 7, 1997.

CASA DEL CORDÓN

Considered the most significant building of Burgos civil architecture, it owes its name to the Franciscan cord that frames its main doorway. It was constructed in the 15th century by Simón de Colonia at the request of the Condestables of Castile, Pedro Fernández de Velasco and Mencía de Mendoza, who also commissioned him with the mortuary chapel in the cathedral. With the passing of the years, new elements would be added, like the Neo-Gothic balconies on the façade, done at the beginning of the 20th century by Vicente Lampérez, and a profound restoration was performed, like those done more recently inside. Today, it houses the central office of the Bank of Burgos, which has a temporary exhibit hall.

Two beautiful towers crowned by artistic ogival ornament flank the elegant main façade, where the doorway and, above all, the coats of arms of the Condestables are found. Surrounding both shields, the Latin inscriptions "A good death honors an entire life", can be read on that of Pedro Fernández de Velasco, and "Everything fades away except the love of God", on that of his wife. The Franciscan cord forms a sober yet pretty tympanum. Inside, the magnificent patio and the no less interesting staircase stand out.

But apart from its unquestionable artistic value, the

Casa del Cordón.

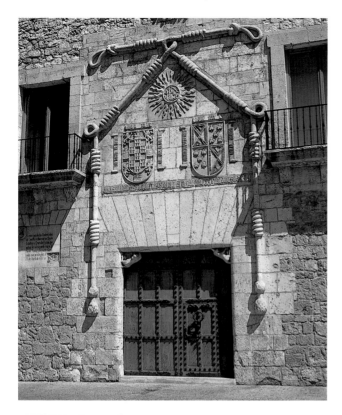

Casa del Cordón: main entrance and detail of the ogival ornament.

Patio of the Casa del Cordón.
Photo ceded by Caja de Burgos.

Casa del Cordón presents richness of historic character. And as the inscriptions of the doorway remind us, here the Catholic Monarchs received Christopher Columbus in 1497 on his return from his second voyage to America. That same year, it was also the setting for the wedding of Prince Juan with Margarita de Austria. Shortly after, in 1506, it witnessed the death of Felipe the Handsome, and in 1515 already, it hosted the meetings of the Courts that made the pact for the union of Navarra and Castile. Other events that took place here in later periods include royal weddings, like that of Felipe IV with Isabel de Borbón, and the temporary presence of monarchs from the Austrian dynasty.

The Casa del Cordón is located in the old plaza del Mercado Mayor (Main Market), today the **plaza de la Libertad** (Liberty) In the past, this public space was one of the nerve centers of Burgos. To its frenetic economic activity, its use as an improvised bullring or solemn decoration of religious processions must be mentioned.

PLAZA OF SAN JUAN

It is a space tightly related to the Way of Saint James. On one side, the **Gate of San Juan** was where the pilgrims and merchants entered the city. On the other side, the current **Marceliano Santa María Museum** and the **Cultural Center** were at one time, the monastery of San Juan, institution founded by Alfonso VI with the idea of assisting the faithful on their way to Santiago. Inside, the work dedicated to Castile by this Burgos painter (1866-1953) can be admired. And the old Hospital of San Juan, of which the doorway is conserved, is today the **Cultural House**. Finally, there is the **church of San Lesmes**.

This temple of beautiful Gothic execution was constructed in the 15th century in honor of San Lesmes, the name by which the French Benedictine monk Adelelmo, who dedicated his life to the most in need, was known by in the city. Passed away in 1097, his kindness and the belief that he performed miraculous cures won him the hearts of the people and with

Plaza of San Juan: Marceliano Santa María Museum, the old Hospital of San Juan (to the right of the image) and statue of Count Diego Rodríguez Porcelos, founder of the city.

Church of San Lesmes.

time, he was declared patron saint of Burgos. Every 30 of January, his festival day, devotees cover his tomb with bread rolls so that the saint can bless them.

The church has three naves, in which elements of Renaissance art appear. Its Baroque high altarpiece, 16th-century pulpit, the gothic tombs on the southern wall, the funerary complex of the chapel of Salamanca and tomb itself of San Lesmes, with a alabaster statue that stands out for its pronounced realism are very interesting.

CHURCH OF SAN GIL

Looking at the outside of this church, nothing calls attention to the fact that you are standing before one of the most beautiful Gothic temples of Castile. The determining factor is the presence on the list of artists who cooperated in its construction, which was completed between the 14th and 16th centuries, the names of great Burgos masters, some of whom also participated in the building of the cathedral.

The church adjoins the medieval wall, accounting for its absence of exterior decoration. However, when entering, the serene grandeur of its interior is immediately apparent, beginning with the majesty of its three naves, sustained upon columns that remind us of the cathedral, and ending with the beautiful tombs, excellent examples of the Gothic and Renaissance styles applied to funerary art. Its chapels deserve a separate chapter. The Nativity chapel from the 16th century is presided over by a Renaissance altarpiece and the fretwork in the central circle is really impressive. The chapel of the Good Morning, so called because of the early hour that its clerics worship there, has a magnificent Gothic altarpiece from the 15th century attributed to Gil de Siloé. According to tradition, Santa Teresa de Jesús would often hear mass here when she came to Burgos to found its last convent of Carmelites. Also interesting is the chapel of the Cross, made by Juan de Vallejo around the second half of the 16th century.

Facing the temple, the **Arch of San Gil**, another gate of the medieval wall that was renovated in the 16th century, is found.

THE PLAZA MAYOR

The distinct urban reforms carried out throughout its history, some a bit arbitrary, have come to confer the Plaza Mayor (Main Square) of Burgos a clearly peculiar aspect. From a bird's eye view, it seems to have an oval shape but in reality it is a deliciously irregular hexagon. The colonnade accentuates, even more if possible, its charm, and its buildings, luxury spectators of a city that daily passes by their feet, are aligned without strident consciousness of their supporting role. The statue of Carlos III, which Alfonso Giraldo Bergaz molded by initiative of the industrialist Antonio Tomé, has presided over the complex since 1784.

In the Plaza Mayor, the **City Hall** has its seat. It was constructed at the end of the 18th century after resolving the doubts about its placement. Finally, it was decided that it should be erected over the arches of the old Gate of the Wagons, next to the Paseo del Espolón. The architect in charge of the project, González de Lara, created a building of neoclassic airs, in which straight lines and rectangular forms predominate. Inside, the sumptuous Session Hall stands out, decorated with paintings by Marceliano Santa María, and the picture by the same artist where El Cid is seen setting off into exile.

The Plaza Mayor was in its day, the plaza del Mercado Menor (Lesser Market). Of its old commercial character, the image of the god Mercury appears in the decoration of one of the building's façades.

Arch of San Gil.

Plaza Mayor.

Main stairway of the Town Hall where the painting of El Cid going into exile is appreciated, work of Marceliano Santa María.

MUSEUM OF BURGOS

Situated on the other bank of the river, on the street Calera, it occupies three noble houses from the 16th century. The well-known Casa Miranda, which houses the sections dedicated to Prehistory and Archeology, is a beautiful Renaissance palace constructed by Juan de Vallejo for Francisco de Miranda. Its artistic doorway, flanked by double classic columns and crowned by the family shields of the property owner, gives way to an interior whose rooms are distributed around a rectangular patio with two floors. In these halls, works of great archeological value, coming from sites of Atapuerca, Ojo Guareña and Clunia are exhibited.

Also by Juan de Vallejo, is the Casa de Íñigo de Angulo, which contains the Fine Arts section of the

Museum of Burgos: set of fragments of diverse skulls proceeding from Atapuerca, set of hatchets proceeding from Ojo Guareña and torsos from the Roman city of Clunia.

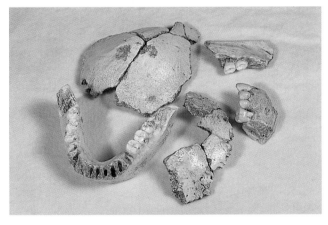

Museum of Burgos: façade of Santo Domingo of Silos.

Museum of Burgos: tomb of Don Juan de Padilla.

Convent of Santa Clara.

museum. Despite its name, it was the ambassador Lope Hurtado de Mendoza who ordered its construction in 1547. Later, it would become the property of Íñigo de Angulo. At an architectural level, it already displays the evolution from Renaissance art to a greater ornamental simplicity. As far as its content, the painted front of the tomb of Santo Domingo de Silos, from the 12th century, the tomb of Don Juan de Padilla done by Gil de Siloé and the painting by Berruguete "Mass of San Gregorio" are the highlights. The third and last house converted into museum is the Casa Melgosa, which has been set aside for Decorative Art and Modern Art.

CONVENT OF SANTA CLARA

Apart from its artistic interest, it has the added value of being the oldest convent in Burgos. Its community of Franciscans was established in the 13th century, after obtaining the papal bull in 1232. The external aspect of the Gothic church possesses great sobriety, while inside, without departing from this line, it offers displays of greater ornamental richness. The altarpieces, done in the 18th century, are especially relevant. Of these, the high chapel, with images of Santa Clara and San Francisco deserve mention. The artistic crossed arch of the sacristy, which represents Jesus Christ crowning the Virgin, is also noteworthy.

OTHER CHURCHES OF THE HISTORIC CENTER

Close to the Plaza Mayor, stands the **church of San Lorenzo**, constructed in the 17th century, the canons of Baroque art are already made manifest in its monumental façade. The interior with Greek cross floor draws an octagon with the chapels set in its walls. Some strong pilasters sustain the majestic cupola with lantern through which the light of the Burgos sky filters. Its high altarpiece, another example of Baroque magnificence, under the charge of the master José Valdán, who executed it in the first third of the 18th century, is interesting too.

The **church of La Merced**, next to the banks of the Arlanzón, was built at the end of the 15th century as part of a convent of Mercedarians. Current parish of the Jesuits, the temple is a clear example of the late Gothic. Inside with three naves, the tombs of Francisco del Castillo and Leonor Pesquera, the matrimony, whose contributions made the construction of the church possible, are found.

Close to the above, the **church of San Cosme and San Damián**, erected between the 15th and the 16th centuries, counts on the intervention of the artist Juan de Vallejo on its doorway. The high altarpiece, with its characteristic Solomon columns, is an excellent Baroque example from the 17th century. On a curious note, many Burgos artists chose this temple for their eternal resting-place.

A little further away from the center, in the district of San Pedro and San Felices, the **convent of Santa Dorotea** was erected at the end of the 15th century. It presents a simple Gothic doorway on its church, work of Simón de Colonia, in which the Catholic Monarchs' coat of arms reign. Inside with just one nave, the high altarpiece and the tombs of Juan de Ortega, first bishop of Almería, and Alonso de Ortega, nephew of the former and elder chaplain of Prince Juan, son of the Catholic Monarchs, stand out. Both tombs are from the beginning of the 16th century and constitute proud examples of the transitional style from Gothic to Renaissance art.

Church La Merced.

Doorway of the church of San Cosme and San Damián.

Royal Monastery of Huelgas: the plaza called Compás de Adentro (Inside Compass), with buildings from the 16th and 17th century. Reproduction authorized by Patrimonio Nacional.

ROYAL MONASTERY OF THE HUELGAS

Away from the center of the city and located in what was until then a place for recreation or "huelga" for the Castillian monarchs, the Royal Monastery of the Huelgas was founded by Alfonso VIII in 1187, although the majority of its construction occurred throughout the 13th century. Besides hosting an influential and important community of Cistercian monks, it served as a royal pantheon and setting for ordination ceremonies for knights of Fernando III, Alfonso XI, Enrique II, Pedro I and Juan II, among other kings.

The building possesses a rich and varied artistic heritage, reflection of the relevance acquired in the past. After crossing a Gothic-styled passage, a plaza is reached, on whose right, distinct rooms of the monastery are aligned. On the left, through an arch,

Arch of entrance to the plaza Compás de Afuera (Outside Compass), behind which the monastery church is distinguished. Reproduction authorized by Patrimonio Nacional.

43

Northern nave of Santa Catalina: tomb of the prince Don Fernando de la Cerda and altarpiece. Reproduction authorized by Patrimonio Nacional.

In the Chapter house paintings from the 15th, 16th and 17th centuries and the famous standard of Las Navas de Tolosa. Reproduction authorized by Patrimonio Nacional.

Standard of Las Navas de Tolosa. Reproduction authorized by Patrimonio Nacional.

45

Hospital of the King.

the silhouette of the temple with its characteristic and defensive strong tower is distinguished. The interior of the church is divided into three long naves, transept and five apse chapels, one large, the central, and four smaller ones to the sides. The magnificent Baroque high altar was done in the middle of the 17th century. The image of the Virgin of the Assumption, framed by beautiful Salomonic columns and the statues of the saints Bernardo and Benito preside over it. In the upper part, there are diverse reliefs with the scenes of Jesus's life and, in the highest part, the images of San Pedro and San Pablo.

Also noteworthy, inside, are the Renaissance, rotating pulpit, which displays an inscription of the year 1560 and the symbols corresponding to the Abbess that ruled the destinies of the monarchs at that time, the simple choir, adorned with French tapestries, and the paintings depicting the Battle of Las Navas de Tolosa, at the end of the 16th century, on the wall that separates the cloister area from the rest of the temple.

In one of the naves, called Santa Catalina, is the Royal Pantheon of the Castillian Dynasty, with the tomb of the infant Fernando de la Cerda in a distinguished place. Another tomb of great artistic and historical interest is the double, gothic-style sarcophagus, where Alfonso VIII and his wife, Leonor of England, who surely was the impulse of the monastery's foundation, are buried. Precisely in the decoration of the king's tomb, the moment when he hands the foundational bull to the monks is immortalized. Likewise, the princess Blanca of Portugal, whose tomb presents details of Mudejar art, Enrique I and his wife Berenguela rest for eternity in this corner.

The monastery has two cloisters, called "The Little Cloisters" and San Fernando. The first is a Roman work from the end of the 12th century, with wooden roof, double pointed arches and artistic capitals. The second is inscribed in Gothic art and it was constructed in the middle of the 13th century. In it, the Mudejar arches ornamented with details of typical Moorish plasterwork stand out.

Other rooms of notable architecture are the chapel of the Assumption, which probably belonged to the royal palace of rest upon which the monastery was built, the chapel of Santiago, where Mudejar artistic elements appear once again in the decoration, and the Chapter house, with its ceiling formed by nine crossed arches that are supported by four pillars. In this last room, we can contemplate paintings from the 15th, 16th and 17th century, some of Flemish origin, and the celebrated standard taken from the Arabs by the Christians in the battle of Las Navas de Tolosa, the 16 of July, 1212, considered the most important of the almost eight centuries of the Re-conquest. The standard was captured from the Almohad leader Abú-Yasuf-Jacub, better known by the Christian troops of the Castillian king Alfonso VIII as Miramamolín. In the festival of Curpillos, the one of the most historic traditions celebrated in Burgos, and that with large popular participation takes place on the Friday following the Sunday of Corpus Christi, the standard is taken out in the procession; nowadays, a copy is paraded. The origins of the festivals point to the commemoration of that transcendental victory that decisively changed the course of the Re-conquest.

The Royal Monastery of the Huelgas also houses one of the best European collections of medieval

Church of Santa María the Royal and Ancient.

fabrics. The pieces, with which the monarchs that rest in its pantheon are buried, make up part of the background.

HOSPITAL OF THE KING

Close to the monastery of the Huelgas, on the other side of the park of Parral, this old hospital, which Alfonso VIII founded for attending the pilgrims travelling on the Way of Saint James, is found. However, little remains of that building today, since the majority of what is conserved corresponds to the work done in the 16th century. The plateresque door of Pilgrims, displays the sitting figure of the apostle Santiago and the shields of Burgos and Castile and Leon on one side, while on the other, there is a sitting image of the Virgin and the coat of arms of Carlos V. Just as interesting are the door that gives access to the church and the façade of the House of the Old

Municipal Charter, The Hospital of the King today is the seat of the University of Burgos.

CHURCH OF SANTA MARÍA THE ROYAL AND ANCIENT

Its origins date back to 1074, the year when Alfonso VI decided to move the bishop of Oca to the current district of Gamonal, then an independent locality situated on the route of the Way of Saint James, a few kilometers from Burgos. Nonetheless, the present, Gothic church from the 14th century has its strong tower from the previous century. The whole building gives a sensation of extraordinary solidity. The powerful buttresses that prop it and the low height of its only nave accentuate this impression even more. A covered portico, in whose tympanum, there is a representation of the Coronation of the Virgin, gives access to a diaphanous space in the form of a Latin cross and square

Carthusian monastery of Miraflores.

Portico of the Carthusian monastery. ▷

CARTHUSIAN MONASTERY OF MIRAFLORES

A few kilometers from Burgos, after leaving the pleasant Paseo de la Quinta behind in direction of the Fuentes Blancas (White Fountains), we find this notable building, from the 15th century, whose interior possesses many elements of marked relevance. Its history begins during the reign of Enrique III, when a palace stood here that he would frequent in order to hunt. In 1441, he decided to cede it to a Carthusian monk community with the aim of founding a monastery under avocation of San Francisco de Asís. After suffering a fire, his son, Juan II, ordered the construction of another convent that would eventually be finished by Queen Isabel the Catholic.

The person in charge of the monumental work was Juan de Colonia, who counted on artists of the stature of his son Simón, Gil de Siloé or Pedro Berruguete to help

him. The first two were the artists of the church, concluded in 1484 but solemnly inaugurated fifteen years later coinciding with the finishing of the high altarpiece. The temple only has one nave, which is accessed by a simple portico in whose tympanum, the scene of Piety is displayed. The coat of arms that crowns it correspond to Juan II and Isabel of Portugal. Inside, the first thing that calls attention is the splendid crossed arch with its very fine ribs of ogival ornament. The so-called Choir of the Laity doesn't wake up any less admiration, with its magnificent Renaissance chairs carved by Simón de Bueras in 1558. Further along, the choir of the Carthusian Fathers displays beautiful choir stalls done by Martín Sánchez at the end of the 15th century.

At the head of the temple, two main attractions of Miraflores are situated. One is the tomb of Juan II and Isabel of Portugal, parents of Isabel the Catholic. Carved in alabaster with impressive virtuosity at the

Carthusian monastery of Miraflores: tomb of Juan II and Isabel of Portugal and tomb of the prince Don Alfonso.

hands of Gil de Siloé between 1489 and 1493, the work has an imposing expressive force. Only looking at the vestments of the Monarchs, which rest over an eight-pointed star, is reason enough for visiting the Carthusian monastery. The other great point of interest is the high altarpiece by the same artist. It was done between 1496 and 1499, and it is said that it was polychrome with part of the gold that Columbus brought from his second voyage to America.

Gil de Siloé again left his indelible stamp on the tomb of the prince Don Alfonso, where the statue of Isabel the Catholic's brother appears praying on his knees before the altar.

The Annunciation of Berruguete, the Baroque statue of San Bruno in the chapel of the same name, carved in wood by the Portuguese Manuel de Pereira in the second quarter of the 17th century, and the Flemish stations of the cross triptych from the 15th century are other authentic marvels that the Carthusian monastery houses.

*High
altarpiece of
the
Carthusian
monastery of
Miraflores.*

*Carthusian monastery of
Miraflores:
"Annunciation" by
Pedro of Berruguete.*

*Carthusian monastery of
Miraflores: Flemish
stations-of-the-cross
triptych.*

Monastery of San Pedro of Cardeña.

MONASTERY OF SAN PEDRO DE CARDEÑA

Ten kilometers separate Burgos from this ancient, Benedictine monastery founded in the year 899 and currently inhabited by Cister monks, who were the silent witnesses of the painful departure of El Cid into exile. Inside these walls and accompanied by his daughters, his wife Doña Jimena served her sentence of exile. The matrimony would later be buried here, where they stayed for centuries until their remains were later moved to the Burgos cathedral. For these and other reasons, the monastery of e San Pedro de Cardeña is known as "the monastery of El Cid".

Even when we find its roots at the close of the 10th century, the majority of the building is the result of an ambitious restoration performed in the 18th century.

Already in the year 953, the troops of Abderramán III had destroyed it, so that it had to be rebuilt in the 11th century. From this period are the tower, from which Doña Jimena scanned the horizon waiting for the return of her husband, and a wing of the cloister of the Martyrs, so called in memory of the monks who were decapitated by the Muslims during the assault of 953. In the 15th century, the gothic church was erected, to which the chapel of El Cid would be added in the 18th century for the Burgos hero and his family. The Chapter house houses diverse paintings by José de Rivera "The Españoleto" and a work by Juan de Juanes.

At the entrance of the monastery, a monolith marks the exact place where Babieca, the legendary horse of El Cid Campeador, is buried.

Monastery of San Pedro of Cardeña: primitive tomb of El Cid.

Presbytery of the monastery. ▷

55

THE ATAPUERCA MOUNTAINS

In 1992, the name of the Atapuerca Mountains, 15 km from Burgos, crossed the borders of Spain when the two best-conserved cranial fossils in the world were found on the so-called Sima de los Huesos (Peak of Bones). A couple of years later, it returned to the spotlight with the discovery in the Gran Dolina of hundreds of human remains whose antiquity is estimated at around 780,000 years. This date brought about the change in the theory that the first hominids to come to Europe form Africa did so about 300,000 years ago.

The discovery of the fossils in the Atapuerca Mountains didn't begin, however, at the close of the 20th century but in that of the 19th. The construction work of mining train infrastructure had already brought diverse remains to light and it wouldn't be long before the interest of scientists awoke. The work of paleoanthropologists would be intensified when in the middle of the last century, more so after 1976, when some of these remains were identified as human fossils.

Declared by UNESCO as a World Heritage Site, the Atapuerca Mountains possess an extraordinary archeological and paleontoligical value. At its three open sites, called Gran Dolina, Galería and Sima de los Huesos, work continues without rest in order to find new clues that would help clarify the stages of human evolution.

Atapuerca: the Gallery site.

Quintanilla de las Villas.

REGION OF ARLANZA

The history of the independent earldom of Castile began to be written in these lands watered by the Arlanza. Each one of the towns in the region keep, in greater or lesser measure, the stamp of those years in which the new political reality was taking shape. Of its author, Count Fernán González, we also find numerous witnesses, at times in the form of stone, at others in the echoes of legend. One of these vestiges is the **Roman abbey of San Quirce**, founded by the Castillian noble and consecrated in 1147. A few kilometers away, and under the protection of the Peña de Lara and the remains of his castle, the town **Quintanilla de las Villas** is found, where the birth in the beginning of the 10th century of Fernán González took place. The remains of the Visigoth shrine of Santa María Virgin, from the end of the 7th century, are its most noteworthy monument.

Already in the valley of the Arlanza itself, next to the riverbank, the remains of the **abbey of San Pedro de Arlanza,** one of the most important Benedictine monasteries of Castile, appear. It was founded in the year 912 by Gonzalo Fernández. His son, the celebrated Fernán González, would die in 970 and would be buried inside its walls next to his wife Doña Sancha, as it had been left said. The Sale of Church Lands by Mendizábal in the 19th century submerged the abbey into chaos and ruin, and many of its pieces were moved to other places. In 1841, the tombs of the first count of independent Castile and his wife found a new space in the ancient collegiate church of Covarrubias. Situated 8 km from San Pedro de Arlanza and 39 from Burgos, the town of **Covarrubias** owes its origin to the son of Fernán González, Count García Fernández, who in the year 978 decided its founding in the application of the politics of repopulating imposed by King Alfonso III the Great. Besides very notable

57

Visigoth shrine of Santa María Virgin, in Quintanilla de las Villas.

Ruins of the abbey of San Pedro of Arlanza.

Covarrubias: Collegiate church of San Cosme and San Damián and Tower of Doña Urraca.

popular architecture and an urban network full of charm that recalls its medieval roots. The town possesses buildings of great interest.

One of these is the collegiate church of San Cosme and San Damián, from the 10th century, although restored in the 15th, In the presbytery, which began to be erected in 1474, Fernán González and his wife Sancha are found in eternal rest, this last one in a 4th century tomb coming from the Roman city of Clunia, near Coruña del Conde. The chapel of the Saint Martyrs, attributed to Juan de Colonia, the tomb of the three Abbess princes called Urraca, and the cloister from the 16th century, a Gothic jewel, where mortal remains of Cristina of Norway, first wife of Prince Felipe, son of Fernando III, are also highlights. Special mention is due the museum, which houses, among other pieces, the triptych of the Adoration of the Three Kings, done at the beginning of the 16th century in a Flemish style by an unknown artist.

Facing the collegiate church, we find the Tower of Doña Urraca, a 22-m high surveillance that was built in the 10th century over the base of a previous one destroyed by the Arabs. Perhaps fruit of its dark aspect, logical on the other hand, if we keep in mind the aim for which it was built. The tower appears linked to the legend of the death by confinement of one Doña Urraca, the name might have belonged to a daughter of Count Fernán González, who got married to three monarchs, or a daughter-in-law of the Count himself, who became a widow shortly after marriage. Neither of the two popular tales clarifies the motive of such a cruel execution. The only thing that doesn't offer any doubt is that the tower constitutes a masterwork of military architecture at the time.

Less mystery surrounds the church of Santo Tomás, another Covarrubias jewel. Although it has a more ancient origin, the current temple dates to the 15th century. Its most noteworthy elements are a Roman

Covarrubias: Archive for the Advancement of Castile and Town Hall.

baptismal font from the 12th century and two altarpieces, one plateresque, from the 16th century, and the other Baroque, from the 18th.

The Archive of the Advancement of Castile is also valuable. It was constructed in 1575 by order of Felipe II for guarding all the documents and writings generated by this institution. A shield of this monarch crowns the façade. The building sits upon an open arch in the medieval wall.

The palace, where, according to tradition, Count Fernán González lived, became the Town Hall, the Palace of the bishop Peña, with its shields and religious distinctions, or the transept situated in front of the Archive, from the 16th century, only reinforce the monumental character of the town of Covarrubias.

Coming from Santo Domingo de Silos, **Santibáñez del Val** possesses the Mozo-Arabic shrine of Santa Cecilia in its municipality. From the 10th century, it presents a squared apse and inside, a triumphal horseshoe arch and semi-spherical cupola. The five arches in the atrium were done in Roman style in the 12th century.

The name of **Santo Domingo de Silos**, 57 km from Burgos, hears the echoes of Gregorian chants and, at the same time, long and profound silences, that have survived for centuries within the walls of its famous monastery. Founded already in the 7th century in the middle of the Visigoth period, it was dedicated in origin to San Sebastián. After it was destroyed by the Arabs, Fernán González ordered it restored around the year 954. However, throughout the 11th century, it would again suffer the consequences of attacks, this time, by the troops of Almanzor. At that time, in 1041, was when the Benedictine monk Domingo arrived to the monastery with the double mission of restoring it and cementing its spiritual prestige. Passed away in 1073, his enormous task would be recognized in the 13th century when his name would forever be associated to that of the monastery.

Even though the totality of the complex possesses an undeniable beauty, the main attraction resides in its cloister. Not in vain, is it considered to be one of the archeological milestones of Roman architecture,

Monastery of Santo Domingo de Silos: presbytery of the church and cloister.

Monastery of Santo Domingo de Silos: detail of the Mudejar coffered ceiling and one of the capitals.

Pharmacy of the Monastery of Santo Domingo de Silos.

Monastery of Santo Domingo de Silos: chapel of Santo Domingo.

General view of Lerma.

not only in Spain but also in the rest of the world. It was constructed between the 11th and 13th centuries and, uncommon for its time, it has two floors. The angles of the lower floor display bas-reliefs with scenes of Jesus Christ's life. On the ceiling, a Mudejar coffered ceiling from the 14th century displays images, some allegorical, of how life was in medieval times. But the highest level of artistic purity is concentrated in the capitals of the double columns that sustain the arches. Except that there were various, there is practically nothing known about the identities of the authors, who carved those stones with extreme mastery until converting them into exponents of myths and mysteries that surround the human condition. Fantastic and real animals, plants and human beings make up a universe of Oriental and Califal thematic symbols, in which some experts believe to see the hands of artists of Muslim origin.

The Neoclassic church of the monastery dates to the second half of the 18th century and is the work of Ventura Rodríguez. Hardly any distinctive remains of the crypt in the primitive Roman temple are con-

served. The reliquaries of Santo Domingo are conserved in an urn of silver in the Baroque chapel that bears his name. A curious pharmacy, founded in 1705, and a museum hold valuable manuscripts, codexes, Visigoth and Roman capitals, the communion cup and paten of Santo Domingo, and diverse pieces of roman origin are also very interesting.

To the west of Santo Domingo de Silos, and 36 km from Burgos, the town of **Lerma** stands above a hill. Authentic compendium of Spanish architecture from the 17th century, its origins date back to the time of the Vacceos, later registering the presence of Romans, Visigoths and Muslims. But the period of greatest prosperity would come to life with Francisco Gómez de Sandoval y Rojas, Duke of Lerma and favorite of King Felipe III. The noble took at the dawn of the 17th century, an ample urban reform beginning with the construction of his own palace and continuing with the building of the church and diverse monasteries, and culminating with the restoration of plazas, streets and the bridge that crosses the river Arlanza. Paradigm of the Duke's ambitious project, the Ducal

Lerma: Ducal Palace and monastery of San Blas.

Palace, was erected between 1601 and 1617 over the ruins of the ancient castle of Lerma. Today, converted into a National Inn of Tourism, it is a building of sober and elegant lines, with four large towers at the ends and a façade presided over by the shields of Sandoval and Rojas. It is found in the spacious, portico Plaza Mayor, which in its day, and fulfilling the desires of the Duke, was filled with mansions, where his relatives resided. Near the palace and united to this by a passageway, the monastery of San Blas was founded in 1613 for housing a community of Dominican monks. Inside, an interesting collection of paintings and carvings, as well as an altarpiece made up of paintings from the beginning of the 16th century, can be admired.

In the plaza of Santa Clara, with its beautiful row of balconies covered by strong arches from which a spectacular view of the fertile plain of the Arlanza can be taken in, the monastery of the Ascension, or convent of Santa Clara, and the convent of Santa Teresa, today the seat of the municipal government, are situated. The first, founded by Santa Clara nuns

Lerma: plaza of Santa Clara and monastery of the Ascension.

Lerma: collegiate church of San Pedro.

in 1605, possesses a splendid gathering of religuaries from the 17th century and paintings by Bartolomé Carducho. The convent of Santa Teresa, with notable façade and cloister, was occupied by Carmelite monks in 1617. In the middle of the plaza, a monument recalls the popular priest Merino, the priest and warrior born in a dependent village of Lerma that gained notoriety by his actions in the War of Independence and in 1852 would be tried for the assassination attempt of Isabel II.

Near the Collegiate Church of San Pedro, there is another emblematic building of Lerma. It was erected between 1613 and 1617, and Felipe III attended its consecration. The three-nave temple with apse-aisle but no transept was generously adorned at the instigation of the Duke of Lerma. Besides its Baroque

high altarpiece and choir stalls, the organ, one of the oldest in Spain, from 1616, and various images, among them, the prayerful statue of the archbishop Cristóbal de Rojas Sandoval, done in golden bronze by Juan de Arfe and Fernández del Moral, are other highlights. The shrine of the Piety, which was the parish of medieval Lerma; the *Humilladero* of Santo Cristo, from the 17th century, the convent of San Francisco of the Kings, which was inhabited by quiet Franciscans; and the monastery of the Mother of God, with a beautiful façade and interesting altarpiece, complete the extensive bill of religious buildings in the town.

Other reforms brought about by the Duke of Lerma, include the medieval bridge and an old gate in the wall, known since then as the Arch of the Prison, since it housed the prison of the locality.

Lerma: medieval bridge and Arch of the Prison.

Canyon of the Lobos River Natural Park, to the south of Salas de los Infantes.

THE ALTA SIERRA

To the east of Burgos, the mountains of Neila and Demanda make up one of the most suggestive natural spaces in the province. These are lands watched over by high peaks, where still lightly travelling rivers flow from, and the dense forests of beech, pine or oak, lakes of waters still like mirrors and the gullies, which were traced by man in their day in order to facilitate the passage of the herds, cast their special magic. These are also lands of ashlar stone houses, with their typical, conical chimneys, narrow, green valleys and towns with medieval flavor.

Salas de los Infantes, 55 km from Burgos, is the capital of the Alta Sierra region. The most interesting monuments of this town founded in the 10th century are the Gothic church of Santa María and the church of Santa Cecilia, which conserves a baptismal font and a Roman-style doorway. A short distance away, **Palacios de la Sierra** possesses one of various high-medieval necropolises that exist in the area. However, what revives greater interest is found in the community of Revenga, the first formed by 133 graves carved in the rock, near the place called La Cerca, and the second in Cuyacabras, outside of **Quintanar de la Sierra**. This town also presents the incentive of its typical mountain residences and the charm of the landscape called Peña el Vaso, where time and nature have molded strange forms in the mountain rock.

Coming from Neila, the relief of the land warns us of our proximity to Lagunas Altas (High Lakes), within the **Natural Park of the Sierra de la Demanda**. Situated at almost 2,000 m in altitude, these small lakes of glacial origin, with the Laguna Negra at the

General view of Salas
de los Infantes.

Necropolis of
Cuyacabras, outside of
Quintanar de la Sierra.

High Lakes, Natural Park of the Sierra de la Demanda.

Neila: palace of the Márquez.

front, make up an authentic natural paradise of moving beauty. The urban nucleus of **Neila** offers another interesting example of traditional architecture, to which the attraction of its ancestral houses must be added. According to tradition, one of these, the palace of Márquez, served as residence and barracks of the popular priest Merino. In the district of San Miguel, is the church of the same name, with apse and tower of Roman style. Important center for pasturing in the past, Neila came to possess a large wool laundry.

Further north, **Barbadillo de Herreros** exhibits the stamp of centuries of prosperity based on the transhumance and blacksmith work. Of the richness generated by the first activity, the numerous emblazoned houses that stand along the streets of the town and that belonged to families integrated in the Honored Council of Mesta are proof. As far as the fame of its ironmongers, it is known that in their workshops,

Barbadillo de Herreros.

many of the swords wielded by the brave Castillian knights were forged here. Among its monuments, the church of San Sebastián, from the 17th century, with a beautiful carving of the saint, attributed to Diego de Siloé.

Following the course of the river Pedroso, the town of **Vizcaínos** appears, leaving no doubt about the origin of its first inhabitants. Its Roman church from the 12th century, consecrated to San Andrés, is its main heritage. The temple of **Jaramillo de la Fuente** is also Roman, with an interesting portico gallery and a Stations of the Cross from the end of the 13th century inside.

Next to the river Arlanzón, **Pineda de la Sierra** is located, an interesting urban area that has a ski station. A privileged setting of beech and holly forests characterize the towns that are situated in this part of the mountain, among which **Pradoluengo** and **Fresneda de la Sierra Tirón** should be cited.

Pradoluengo.

Town Hall of Briviesca.

THE BUREBA

Exceptional witness of the beginning of Castillian history, the Bureba is an eminent agricultural region situated in the northeast of the province, where art and nature melt together to offer images of great beauty. Before fully entering it, you should stop at the **Monastery of Rodilla** and see the shrine of Our Lady of the Valley, a Roman building from the 12th century, which forms part of the monastery that gives its name to the town. Overlooking the shrine, there are the remains of a 10th century castle that in the 14th century became the property of the Velasco family. **Briviesca**, the capital of Bureba, is an elegant locality, whose origins are found in the nearby mountain of San Juan. There, a Celtic-Iberian town, of the Autrigon tribe, who the Romans called Virobesca, from which it derives its present name, became an important Roman crossroads. But in 1387, its name gained certain notoriety with the holding of the General Courts

of Castile. In that historic meeting, it was agreed that the title Prince of Asturias would be awarded to the inheritors of the Castillian throne. Briviesca enjoyed even greater prosperity in the 16th century, period when many of the emblazoned houses that populate its streets were built.

The city map of Briviesca has a square structure that gravitates around the spacious Plaza Mayor with colonnade. The Town Hall resides here, occupying the old palace of Soto Guzmán. Here too, the silhouette of the church of San Martín rises, with its plateresque doorway, its Gothic and Renaissance tombs and its Baroque altarpiece.

A noteworthy monument is the convent of Santa Clara, which houses what is considered to be one of the most notable high altarpieces of the Spanish Renaissance. Dedicated to the Virgin, it was done in walnut by Diego de Guillén, who initiated it in 1550, and Pedro López de Gámiz. In its five sections, scenes of the lives of the Mother of God, Jesus the

Briviesca: plateresque doorway of the church of San Martín.

Briviesca: House of the Salamanca and Collegiate church of Santa María.

Briviesca: convent of Santa Clara, high altarpiece and starred vault of the main chapel.

Apostles and various saints appear. Another attraction of this convent, constructed by Gil de Ontañón and Pedro de Resines in the middle of the 16th century is the magnificent starred vault that covers the main chapel. Close to the convent are a Gothic temple with three naves and a Renaissance façade with a valuable altarpiece, which López de Gámiz also worked on.

10 km from Briviesca the **sanctuary of Santa Casilda**, from the 16th century, stands over a steep landscape. To the artistic value of the complex, that without a doubt the image of the namesake carved by Diego de Siloé contributes, the beauty of the surrounding must be added. Daughter of the Sultan of Toledo, Santa Casilda was in life a good-hearted princess who secretly distributed bread among the hungry Christian prisoners. Surprised one day by her father and interrogated about the contents of her basket, the youth responded with security that there were only flowers. When opened to the incredulous eyes of the Sultan, the miracle occurred and instead of bread, roses appeared. After this incident, the princess abandoned Toledo and came to live in these lands of Burgos.

To the west of the region, **Poza de la Sal** has known economic prosperity for a very long time thanks to the exploitation of its salt mines. If the Romanization already left a special mark on the town, the Middle Ages represented a golden period, which was initiated in the 10th century with the construction of the castle and the wall and would continue with the concession of the municipal charters in 1136 on behalf of Alfonso VII. Lord of Rojas since the end of the 13th century, Carlos V awarded Juan de Rojas the title of Marquis of Poza in 1530.

Despite the passing of many years, Poza de la Sal conserves that charm so peculiar of medieval towns. In its very old but very well conserved walls, three gates are opened: the High Gate, the Gate of the Ages and the Gate of the Conjurer, which was the main one. In 1694, a balcony was added to this last one, from which the priest conjured the clouds, the reason for its name. Adjacent to the wall, the Town Hall is a sober building from the 18th century, Nearby, the Gothic church of San Cosme and San Damián, with a notable Baroque doorway, houses three splendid altarpieces, two from the 16th century, dedicat-

Sanctuary of Santa Casilda.

General view of Poza de la Sal.

Poza de la Sal: Gate of the Conjurer and church of San Cosme and San Damián.

Poza de la Sal: old installations of the salt mines.

Ojeda.

Oña: Plaza Mayor and monastery of San Salvador.

ed to San Andrés and the Virgin of the Rosary, and the third from the 18th.

Outside this walled area, the House of the Administration of Salt Mines was built in the 18th century with the object of regulating the lucrative activities related to this product. Some of the installations used until the middle of the past century for the exploitation of salt continues standing to this day. Found in worse condition is the Castle of Rojas, but the panorama that can be contemplated from its heights compensates the effort of the climb.

Between Poza de la Sal and Oña, stretches the **Valley of Caderechas**, a small valley full of natural charms, especially in the spring. A visit to the distinct towns that are found in it allow you to discover the simple charm of its popular architecture and interesting constructions like the Tower of the Princes in **Ojeda** or the shrine of Santo Ángel in **Hozabejas**.

Oña, situated on the slopes of the mountain of Llana, is another important nucleus of the region. Oña acquired notoriety in the 11th century with the foundation of the

Benedictine monastery of San Salvador. Today converted into a medical center, this ancient abbey was one of the most powerful in Castile. Proof of this is in its church, in both tombs of wood magnificently carved by fray Pedro de Valladolid at the end of the 15th century, rest for eternity García Sánchez, the last count of Castile, King Sancho the Elder of Navarra and King Sancho II of Castile. In the cloister, below some Gothic-style arches, the counts of Bureba are buried.

The monarchal complex is of considerable proportions. Its enormous Baroque façade dates to the 17th century, when notable restoration was performed. The choir stalls, the Chapter house, which holds authentic artwork, and the circular tower of the clock, whose origin dates back to the 10th century, are its most impressive elements.

Of Oña's medieval past, which had an important Jewish community, remains of the walls, some towers and one of the gates, called the Arch of the Star, are conserved. The gothic church of San Juan is also interesting, built between the 12th and 15th centuries and restored in the 16th.

The Bureba is a region with rocky landscapes, small valleys and rivers. Paradigm of it all is the **narrow mountain pass of the Horadada**, which goes from Oña to the Mountain of Tesla and a very short distance from the point where the Ebro and the Oca come together. At a historical level, it should be noted that the narrow mountain pass of the Horadada was one of the most utilized passes for the Muslims in their persistent raids or incursions, in the 9th and 10th centuries, when Castile was born, a matter that the Muslims wisely judged as dangerous, since it was precisely Castile that ended up leading the fight that ended with the expulsion of the Muslims from the Peninsula. From the castles that crown the Mountain of Tesla, especially from the castle of Tedeja, near **Trespaderne**, today under excavation, the Christians saw the arrival of the Arabs and pre-

Frías.

Frías: castle and church of San Vicente.

pared their defense. These castles, in large measure, were responsible for the naming of "Castile", which means "land of castles".

Further north, **Frías** stands out over the slope of a hill protected by a castle on its heights that began to be constructed there in the 12th century. However, the origin of the town is before, as demonstrated by a document of donation from the year 867, in which its name appears. A place of passage for those who from Bureba went to the north of Spain, the town lived its most golden period during the Middle Ages. From the one-time powerful castle of Frías, some of its walls remain standing, with windows decorated with Roman capitals, and the imposing tower of Tribute, visible from many kilometers away. Inside the urban center already, the church of San Vicente was the most relevant of the five existing temples of its day. It has three Gothic naves, edified between the 13th and 14th centuries, and two side chapels, the first

dedicated to Christ of the Temptations, from the 14th century, and the second, the Visitation, from the 16th century. Its splendid Roman doorway was moved to the Museum of the Cloisters in New York after the collapse of the tower in 1904. In the same period, is the church of San Vitores, of which only the doorway and part of its structure are conserved. Review of the monumental heritage of Frías wouldn't be complete without mentioning the convents of Santa María del Vadillo, from the 13th century, and San Francisco, from the 14th.

1 km from Frías, and uniting the two banks of the Ebro, a bridge of Roman origin is found, over which the present one was erected in the medieval period. The majestic defensive tower there in the middle dates to the 14th century. Simpler, but not less interesting is the medieval bridge of **Tobera**, next to the shrines of Christ and Our Lady of the Gorge.

Medieval bridge, outside of Frías.

Pancorbo.

MIRANDA DE EBRO AND THE COUNTY OF TREVIÑO

The northeast of the Burgos province has traditionally been a nexus of union between the interior of Spain and the area of Cantabria. Conscientious of its strategic value, Arabs and Christians fought fierce battles in the 9th century in order to control it. Especially hard were the battles fought around the castle of **Pancorbo**, which stands on the heights of the impressive narrow pass of the Obarenes Mountains. Seeing the wildness and the narrowness of the pass, the reasons for considering the castle the "gateway of Castile" are obvious. Today, only a few remains of the fort are standing, despite the reconstruction carried out in the 16th and 18th centuries. Inside the town, the church-

es of Santiago, which houses a notable Renaissance altarpiece, and San Nicolás, with its medieval tower and Gothic parochial Cross, stand out. In the surroundings, and in what was one of the secondary routes of the Way of Saint James, the shrines of Christ of the District and Our Lady of the Way are found.

Leaving the narrow pass, the small village of **Encío** is located, with its beautiful Roman church of San Cosme and San Damián. Close by, **Santa Gadea del Cid** is a pretty locality of medieval flavor that in the 9th century was known by the name of the Limits for being situated between the kingdoms of Castile and Navarra. The remains of an 11th century castle preside over this picturesque urban area. Today, two of the ancient wall's gates, the Gothic church of San Pedro and, on the other side of the ravine, the Roman

Santa Gadea del Cid.

shrine of Our Lady of Ages, from the 12th century, are visible. In the surroundings of Santa Gadea, the monastery of Our Lady of the Thorn, whose foundation dates back to 1410, is found.

Coming from Miranda de Ebro, the Monument to the Shepherd greets those who are going to **Ameyugo**, another town of medieval origin, where the Tower of the Guevara is the highlight.

Miranda de Ebro, the second most important capital of the province, has constituted, from ancient times, a vital knot of connections. Due to this, it soon gained notable economic development based primarily on trade, and with the passing of the centuries, on industry. The key of this prosperity lies in the bridge that

Ameyugo: Monument to the Shepherd.

85

Miranda de Ebro: bridge of Carlos III.

unites the two banks of the river Ebro, an obligatory passage for people and merchandise that were headed to La Rioja or Álava from Castile and vice versa. Although the origins of Miranda de Ebro date back to the time of the Celts, the current city rose out of the 11th century due to the repopulating imposed by Count García Ordóñez and the concession, on behalf of Alfonso VI, of its municipal charter. The urban nucleus of the town was formed by two districts, Aquende and Allende, well marked by the riverbank. The first, and older, was under the protection of the castle that was elevated upon the mountain of Picota, of which there are hardly any remains. On this bank, we can admire the Gothic church of San Juan Bautista, from the 14th century, the church of Santa María, from the 16th, the seat of Town Hall that Ventura Rodríguez constructed in 1778; and various stately houses from the 16th century that display the coats of arms of their owners.

In the district of Allende, the church of San Nicolás

Town Hall of Miranda de Ebro.

Miranda de Ebro: church of San Juan Bautista and detail of the apse of the church of San Nicolás.

Miranda de Ebro: church of Santa María.

La Puebla de Arganzón.

or the Holy Spirit is situated, edified between the 12th and 13th centuries, presenting a beautiful doorway halfway between Roman and Gothic and an apse whose style leans toward the Roman. Symbol of the city, the bridge of Carlos III is a work from the 18th century that exhibits two lions with both shields of the King and Miranda de Ebro in the central part.

Surrounded by Alaves lands, the County of Treviño appears tied to the province of Burgos since it was conquered at the end of the 12th century by Alfonso VIII and integrated into the crown of Castile. This very monarch founded **La Puebla de Arganzón** and conceded it its municipal charter there in the year 1191. The town, located on the banks of the Zadorra, is crossed by what was then a busy secondary route of the Way of Saint James that left from Vitoria. Its most important monument is the church of Our Lady of the Ancient, constructed between the 14th and 15th centuries and later restored. Inside, an enor-

mous high altarpiece of Renaissance style from the 16th century stands out.

In the center of **Treviño**, its capital is found. Founded by Sancho VI of Navarra in 1151 and incorporated into Castile in 1199, the town revolves around the church of San Pedro. The temple, which was erected in the 13th century following the guidelines of the Gothic, possesses a Baroque tower, an altarpiece from the 18th century and a Gothic carving of Jesus Crucified. In one of its outside corners, the image of the White Virgin is observed.

5 km from Treviño, in **San Vicentejo**, the most valuable artistic treasure of the county is found. It is the Roman shrine from the 12th century, with only one nave, a precious apse with five arches and capitals decorated with vegetable motifs. In the surroundings of **Laño,** the highlight is the existence of a complex of caves, inhabited in their day by hermits, which has its origin in the Visigoth period.

Treviño.

San Vicentejo: Roman shrine.

Valley of Valdivieso.

THE MERINDADES AND THE MOUNTAIN ROUTE

The north of the province is characterized by the presence of spacious areas of mountains, where rivers like the Ebro, the Nela or the Trueba have sometimes carved wide and evocative valleys and at other times steep, narrow mountain passes. Part of this territory corresponds to what is called Merindades, name given to the political-administrative divisions created in the 10th century, in which the merino took charge of administering justice by order of the king. In 1560, Felipe II designated Villarcayo judicial center of the Merindades of Castile, a capitalness that, with other connotations, today still enjoys and projects over the rest of the northern regions.

In order to arrive to Villarcayo, 75 km from Burgos, you have to enter the **Valley of Valdivieso**. Boundaries drawn by the mountains of Tesla and Tudanca, those privileged natural setting, through which the waters of the Ebro flow down, offers images of great beauty, many of them perfectly visible from the heights of the gate of Mazorra. This unbeatable vantage point, also allows seeing, further away, the country homes of towns like **Valdenoceda**, with its Roman church from the 12th century and the medieval tower of Velasco, **Quintana de Valdivieso**, watched over for centuries by the tower of Loja, **El Almiñe**, where we find the interesting, initially Roman, temple of San Nicolás, or **San Pedro de Tejada**, one of the most beautiful and best conserved Roman churches of the province.

Passing **Bisjueces**, where according to tradition, the first judges of Castile laid sentence, **Medina de Pomar**, a beautiful city full of history, appears on the horizon, which today has become a first class summering center. Probably founded by Mozo-Arabs in the 10th or 11th century, the town gained its municipal charters in the 12th century and rapid economic development, thanks to commercial and artesian activities. Under the dominion of the Velasco's, to which King Enrique II had given the town, it was the capital of the Merindades and reached its highest level of wealth. It is precisely the Citadel that Pedro Fernández de Velasco ordered built in the 14th century that would dominate the city's profile. Its strong and austere towers contrast with the exquisite delicacy that the frieze of Mudejar plasterwork presents on the first floor. The Holy Cross church nearby, erected between the 13th and 15th centuries, took advantage of a portion of the wall. Fragments of this wall, as well as some of its gates and arches, remain standing.

The convent of Santa Clara is the most valuable monument of Medina. Sancho Sánchez de Velasco founded it in 1313 and with time, it would become one of the most powerful monasteries in Castile. The Chapel of the Conception with its starred vault, very similar to the chapel of the Condestables in the Cathedral of Burgos, and a magnificent Baroque altarpiece from the 16th century by Felipe de Vigarny, are noteworthy. This place was chosen by the Velasco family to be buried. The alabaster statues of the mausoleum of Íñigo Fernández de Velasco and his wife demand admiration. The convent museum, with pieces like a splendid Flemish table or a Crucifixion of Lepanto elaborated in marble, is an obligatory visit. Next to Santa Clara, stands the Hospital of Veracruz, from

Valdenoceda: tower of the Velasco and Roman church of San Miguel.

The Citadel of Medina de Pomar.

Medina de Pomar: the Town Hall, in the Plaza Mayor.

Medina de Pomar: Convent of Santa Clara and mausoleum of Íñigo Fernández de Velasco.

the 15th century, and the Roman shrine of Santa Lucía or San Millán, from the 12th.

Villarcayo, capital of the Merindades since the 16th century, is another important summering locality today, marked by ancestral homes that denote its time of glory. Its monumental heritage doesn't shine like it should due to fires and sackings that it suffered during the First Carlist War. Its main center of interest is the Museum-monastery of Santa María the Royal of Vileña, moved here from Bureba after being devoured by the flames in 1970. Among its most valuable works, the gothic tombs of Doña Urraca, founder of the monastery, and the Rojas family, the remains of a Mudejar coffered ceiling and various historic documents stand out.

A few kilometers to the west, we have the opportunity to contemplate one of those surprises that, once in a while, nature gives us: a large rock that has been transformed into a spectacular natural bridge provoked by the erosion caused by the river Nela, upon which the town of **Puentedey** sits.

Coming from Espinosa de los Monteros, a detour leads us to **Cueva de Sotoscueva**. A short distance

Puentedey.

from the town, we find the shrine of the saints Tirso and Bernabé, constructed in one of the mouths of the Carstic complex of "Ojo Guareña", the largest of these characteristics in Spain, to the astonishment of visitors.

Surrounded by suggestive mountain landscapes, **Espinosa de los Monteros** is an important commercial locality, whose roots go back to the 9th century. In 1006, the epithet of "Los Monteros" was added because of an inhabitant of the town who discovered a plot to assassinate the Count of Castile, Sancho García. The count then decide to create the institution of "Los Monteros", which would be formed by the noblemen and natives of Espinosa. Included among the privileges and honors that it had was that of keeping watch over the chamber of the kings of Castile at night, a tradition that was continued until 1931.

The stately houses are a constant in the city map of Espinosa. Those of the Marquis of Chiloeches, from the 17th century; the Condestables, Baroque; the Carrillo del Hoyo, which still conserves some battlements from the 15th century original or the Monteros, where the original Gothic work lives together with the restoration performed later, stand out. As far as its churches, the oldest is that of San Nicolás, even though it was very much restored in the 18th century. The church of Santa Cecilia, in the portico Plaza Mayor, was erected in the 16th.

On the other bank of the Trueba, the large tower of the castle of the Condestables or the Velasco's solemnly emerges, a somber yet beautiful building erected between the 14th and 15th centuries.

This entire area is prodigious in valleys, dreamed of natural settings and old paths where the steps of the Roman soldiers still seem to be heard. Landscapes like **Las Machorras**, with its typical country homes, or the **Valley of Mena**, the only one of the Burgos territories whose river empties into the Cantabrian Sea, are a few of the infinite charms that are worth discovering. Small towns with notable examples of

94

Carstic complex of "Ojo Guareña": drain of the river Guareña.

popular, civil and religious architecture aren't lacking. Synthesis of this symbiosis is the locality of **Villasana de Mena**, where, besides the Tower of the Velasco, from the 13th century, the Roman relief of the church of Our Lady of the Altices and the convent of Santa Ana, from the end of the 15th century.

In the Valley of Mena, and in Valdegobía, a town situated on the boundary with Alava, was where the first repopulating took place that at the beginning of the 9th century began to configure and order the territory that would be come Castile. Here, in the Valley of Mena, the Monastery of Taranco was founded, of which only a commemorative monument barely remains, where the word "Castile" was written for the first time.

Cave of Sotoscueva: shrine of the saints Tirso and Bernabé.

General view of Espinosa de los Monteros.

Espinosa de los Monteros: House of the Marquis of Chiloeches and castle of the Velasco.

Country home in Las Machorras.

Valley of Mena: Relloso.

General view of Sedano.

VALLEY OF SEDANO AND THE LORAS

The landscape to the northeast of Burgos is indebted to the patient work that was brought about during thousands of years by the rivers Ebro and Rudrón. Once more, the province of Burgos surprises us with beautiful natural corners, not exempt of interesting contrasts. These lands are also full of history, a history that can be read in the stones of its towns and in the echoes of its legends.

Sedano, 47 km from Burgos, is the capital of the valley of the same name. The country home, so characteristic of this northern area, is presided over by the church of Santa Maria, which holds the image of the Morenita, patron saint of Sedano. Its numerous palatial houses, like that of Bustillo, from the 17th century, tell us of past times full of splendor. Very close to this locality, in **Moradillo de Sedano**, the contemplation of the Roman temple of San Esteban can be enjoyed and check out the similarities between its doorway and the famous portico of Glory of the Cathedral of Santiago de Compostela. Perhaps by the same author, is the Roman temple of **Gredilla de Sedano**, another brilliant example of religious art at the end of the 12th century,

Situated in the canyon of the Rudrón, **Covanera** returns the visitor's attention to the creative power of nature, due to the presence of curious rock formations of Carstic origin. In a no less suggestive setting, **Valdelateja** constitutes the gateway to the imposing canyon of the Ebro, the point where this river and the Rudrón magically meet. This narrow pass, which continues up to **Pesquera**, is one of the most attractive landscapes in the entire province. From Pesquera, whose origins date back to the 9th century, its numerous country houses, the temple San Sebastián and the medieval bridge stand out.

Architecture recuperates its protagonism in **Escalada**, with buildings like the Roman church of the Assumption. Neighbor of the above, **Orbaneja del Castillo** is erected for convincing reasons in a picturesque locality. Its houses appear surrounded by a series of crags with whimsical shapes, more appropriate of a dream world rather than the real one, as if this natural barrier had been capable of detaining time. Today you can read street names with Mozo-Arabic reminiscences: Almotacén or Almojahada.

Sedano: house of the Bustillo.

Covanera: the Pozo Azul (Blue Well).

Valdelateja.

Orbaneja del Castillo.

Villahoz.

THROUGH THE HIGH MOORS OF BURGOS

The extensive fields of cereals are the absolute owners of the western lands of the province. There, where the horizon appears to lose itself into infinity and the landscape becomes definitively Castillian, there are a good number of towns where adobe architecture lives in perfect harmony with luxurious palaces and large churches. The first example of this happy coexistence is found in **Villahoz**. Its enormous temple of the Assumption from the 16th century, houses three magnificent Baroque altarpieces from the 18th century. The church of San Miguel, in **Mahamud**, also has considerable dimensions, and where, in 1507, Jiménez de Cisneros received the Cardenalate at the hands of Fernando the Catholic. Erected between the 14th and 16th centuries, it possesses interesting Renaissance altarpieces, a baptismal font from the 13th century and a Mudejar pulpit. The preponderant part that Mahamud played long ago is given account in the jurisdictional roll in the Plaza Mayor.

Situated just 3 km from the above, **Santa María del Campo** lived its golden years under the reign of Felipe the Handsome and Doña Juana, since they often spent time in this town. Its name is also related with the church of the Assumption, a magnificent building that was erected between the 13th and 16th centuries and that features a plateresque tower, work of Diego de Siloé, considered by some experts to be the most beautiful of the entire Spanish Renaissance. The choir stall, the Mudejar pulpit, the altarpieces, the Flemish tapestries and the tombs add to this attraction. Santa María del Campo still conserves a portion of the ancient wall, three of its gates and various emblazoned houses.

If we continue the thread of history, we find **Los Balbases**, another town with medieval flavor, where Queen Doña Berenguela took care of the sons of Alfonso X the Wise, or **Pampliega,** where the already dethroned monarch Wamba died.

These lands have also seen pilgrims, who over the

Santa María del Campo: church of the Assumption.

centuries traveled the Way of Saint James. Many of the localities that are found along the pilgrimage route took advantage of this circumstance in order to develop themselves. Paradigm of the value of being a place of obligatory passage is observed in **Castrojeriz**, town of Celtic-Iberian origin that in its day came to have seven hospitals. As occurs in similar cases, its urban map is divided between both sides of the main street, and what amounts to the same, along what is the Way of Saint James. Of its monuments, the excollegiate church of Santa María del Manzano, from the 13th century, with a notable image of its namesake, the church of Santo Domingo, from the 16th century, with an important museum; the Roman tower of the church of San Juan; or the convent, which Alfonso X founded and dedicated to Santa Clara, are the highlights.

Villasandino is another nucleus that shone with its own light during the Middle Ages. Its two large churches, one consecrated to the Assumption and the other to the Nativity, and the bridge from the 13th century over the river Odra are its main monuments. A few kilometers away, the indubitable silhouette of

General view of Castrojeriz.

*Castrojeriz:
church of San
Juan and Casa
del Cordón.*

*Castrojeriz:
excollegiate
church of Santa
María del
Manzano.*

Fortress of Olmillos de Sasamón.

the castle that the Cartagena family ordered built in the middle of the 15th century tells us that we are in **Olmillos de Sasamón**. Besides the fort, which conserves its various circular towers, its battlements and the patio of arms in good condition, the parochial church of the Assumption, with a Baroque altarpiece presided over by an image of the Virgin from the 14th century, stands out.

Romanization also arrived, and in an important way, to these Burgos lands and localities. Few, however, can boast of having had the very Caesar Augustus himself as a neighbor during some time. And this occurred in **Sasamón**, the ancient pre-Roman Segisama, from which the first Roman emperor in history led the wars against the Cantabrians and Asturians around the year 25 BC. In the Middle Ages, the town continued having considerable weight. The church of Santa María the Royal, with its cathedral airs, demonstrates this. Constructed in the 13th century, it is made up of five naves and transept, and has a beautiful doorway,

inspired by the Sarmental of the Cathedral of Burgos. The western door, in transition from Roman to Gothic, is older. In the 16th century already, the door of San Miguel was constructed. Inside, the carving of the Archangel San Miguel, by Diego de Siloé; the image of the church's namesake, from the 15th century, the valuable altarpieces, from the 16th, or the cloister, where Juan de Colonia worked, are noteworthy. Remains of the medieval wall, some emblazoned houses and the Plaza Mayor, from 1781, complete the tour through the artistic heritage of Sasamón.

A few kilometers to the north of Sasamón, the imposing **Peña Amaya** (crag Amaya) inspires awe. There was the capital of the Cantabria that Augustus defeated, which had the same name as the crag, and in the surroundings, the Roman Emperor led the first advances of his legions. **Amaya** is one of the places of greater historical density in Spain: besides its Roman past, the Visigoth King Leovigildo converted it into the capital of the Dukedom of Cantabria, after sub-

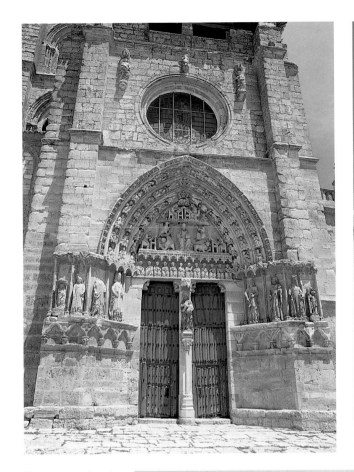

Sasamón: church of Santa María the Royal and Arch at entrance to the town.

Peña Amaya.

jecting the indomitable Cantabrians, who had torn their territory away from the rest of Spain due to the fall of the Roman Empire. Likewise, when the Muslims invaded the Peninsula in 711, the Visigoth nobles, seeing what was approaching, fled towards Amaya with all their treasures. Tarik, the Muslim leader, chased them there, and once the fortress fell, the Gothic nobles received the knife and their treasures were pillaged (the Visigoths were known for their gold craftsmanship). Later still: in the same repopulating impulse that Alfonso III set in motion in 860, cities like Astorga and Leon came back to life. In Castile, it was Amaya that played the part of launch pad for Christian expansion. Today, the place is barely a melancholy evocation of what it was, and only a few stones here and there belie the magnificence of its historic past.

Near Sasamón, **Villadiego** is a town founded by Count Diego Porcelos in the 18th century. It is a place that many Spanish people have evoked on more than one occasion without ever having set foot in it. The reason of this apparent contradiction lies in the extensive use of the popular saying "tomar las de Villadiego" ("take to Villadiego") which means leave running. According to the explanation with greatest glint of credibility, the origin of the expression comes from the persecution that the Jews suffered in the 13th century, harassment that the Hebrew community that lived in Villadiego were saved from due to the privilege granted by King Fernando III. So, the Jews, who wanted to escape the harassment, only had to go to the locality, or "take to Villadiego".

At the margin of popular sayings, the town has earned deserved fame for its numerous monuments. Its nerve center is the Plaza Mayor, which is presided over by the statue of the Agustine historian Enrique Flórez, native of the town and artist of the masterwork *España Sagrada* (Sacred Spain). The plaza connects with the Arch of the Prison, one of medieval wall

Plaza Mayor of Villadiego.

Villadiego: Arch of the Prison and church of Santa María.

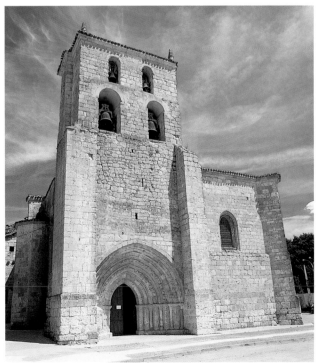

gates, which today, houses an interesting museum of painting. Near the museum, is the convent of San Miguel, which was erected over the ancient Jewish synagogue. Its church, from the 16th century, holds a marvelous altarpiece also from the 16th century. The church of Santa María, from the 16th century and with remains from the 13th, the church of San Lorenzo, with Roman doorway, and the palace of the Condestables, from the 17th century, are also notable. At the boundary with Palencia, the town of **Melgar de Fernamental** is situated. Among its monuments are the noble houses of Cordón and Palazuelos, and the church of the Assumption, from the 16th century, which has a gothic image of the Virgin with the Christ child. Outside of Melgar, we have the opportunity to see one of the greatest works of civil engineering of the 18th century, the Canal of Castile, whose construction lasted about a hundred years and it had a large influence in the commercial development of the region.

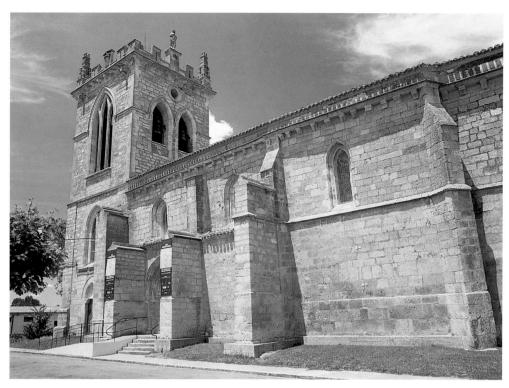

*Villadiego: church of
San Lorenzo and palace
of the Condestables.*

Town Hall of Melgar de Fernamental.

Canal of Castile.

Vineyards in Aranda del Duero.

THE RIBERA DEL DUERO

Talking about the south of the province means talking about land of pronounced personality, in which the river Duero and wine form an inseparable combination full of flavors, aromas and colors. Almost three-quarters of the vineyards of the entire Ribera del Duero, which stretches through other Castile-Leon provinces, are within this Burgos region, whose capital is **Aranda del Duero**. Situated about 80 km from Burgos, the origins of Aranda date back to the pre-Roman period, although it wasn't until the Middle Ages that it would gain notable development. At the end of the 15th century, thanks to its help to the cause of Isabel the Catholic in her push for succession to the Castillian throne, the town enjoyed privileges that would soon be captured in its monumental heritage. Coinciding with these years of splendor, the highly admired main door was erected for the church of Santa María, constructed in the 15th century in late Gothic style over the remains of a previous Roman temple, of which one of its towers is still conserved.

Attributed to Simón de Colonia, the doorway, profusely adorned, possesses an altarpiece structure where numerous figures, scenes of Jesus's life and passages from the Passion appear. In the highest part, the shields of the Catholic Kings and the town dominate. Inside, illuminated by the light that penetrates the three beautiful rose windows, the choir staircase, from the 16th century, and the pulpit and the high altarpiece, both Renaissance pieces, and the chapel of the Salazar stand out.

A few meters away, stands the Gothic church of San Juan. Apart from its notable doorway from the 14th century, the chapel of the Calderonas, with an excellent plateresque altarpiece from the 16th century, stands out. Another building that awakes interest in Aranda is the palace of the Berdugo, from the 15th century. In the surroundings already, the Arandans have an important center of devotion in the sanctuary of their patron saint, the Virgin of the Vineyards.

Outside of **La Vid,** we find the monastery of Santa María de la Vid, founded in the 12th century by the followers of San Norberto in the place, where, according to tra-

Aranda de Duero: main doorway of the church of Santa María.

111

Aranda de Duero: doorway of the church of San Juan and palace of the Berdugo.

dition, the carving of this Virgin was discovered. The Chapter house, from the time the building was built, and the Baroque façade of the church, which ended in 1728, is interesting. The library of the monastery, today occupied by Augustines, holds valuable codexes among its more than 40,000 volumes.

Seven kilometers to the north, the silhouette of **Peñaranda de Duero** tells us that we find ourselves before one of the most beautiful towns of the region. In the heights of the slopes, upon which the country home sits, the proud tower of Tribute of the castle of the Avellaneda sticks out. Although its origins are earlier, the fortress that we see today is from the 15th century. The urban center of Peñaranda maintains a live record of what it was in its day, an important ducal town. This is seen in the Plaza Mayor, where the palace of the Zúñiga and Avellaneda and the excollegiate church of Santa Ana stand. From the beginning of the 16th century, the palace exhibits a splendid plateresque doorway that, once crossed, leads us into an elegant double arcade patio. From here, the distinct rooms are distributed, some of which proudly display Gothic, Mudejar and Renaissance coffered ceilings. The church, for its part, is also from the 16th century. It is curious observing the three busts and diverse columns adorning its Baroque façade, which came from the neighboring Roman town of Clunia. The plaza, from where we can see various fragments of the ancient medieval wall, is presided over by a jurisdictional roll of Gothic design.

Another point of interest in Peñaranda is the Botica of the Jimeno. Opened at the end of the 17th century, the pharmacy, one of the oldest in Spain, possesses a good number of jars, mortars, pots and books that the distinct generations of Jimeno's have conserved with extraordinary zeal.

From **Coruña del Conde,** the echoes of the feat that protagonized the close of the 18th century by one of its inhabitants, Diego Marín, who with bravery and a rudimentary gadget, was able to fly a few meters after jumping from a mountaintop. The other attraction of the locality is more traditional, a shrine from the end of the 11th century or the beginning of the 12th, which possesses various worked stone pieces from nearby Clunia.

With a population of about 30,000 inhabitants, **Clunia** was one of the most important Roman cities in the north of the Peninsula. The fact that it wouldn't be urbanized until after it was abandoned in the 4th century has left infinite remains and ruins to be discovered, giving a fairly precise idea of its preponderant

Peñaranda de Duero: Plaza Mayor and palace of the Avellaneda.

Peñaranda de Duero: medieval wall.

Clunia: theater and mosaic.

part during the Romanization of Iberia. Here, the general Sertorio firmly stood in defiance to Pompey, who wouldn't hesitate in destroying it around the year 75 BC. In 68 AC already, it saw how Servio Sulpicio Galba revolted against Nero and proclaimed himself Emperor of Rome. Historical matters aside, in Clunia, the ruins of buildings like the forum, the imperial thermal baths, the theater carved in rock, which is one of the largest on the Peninsula, and diverse houses with mosaics can be admired.

The tour through this region continues in **Caleruega**, the town that bore witness to the birth in 1170 of Santo Domingo de Guzmán, founder of the Dominican Order and patron saint of the province. Next to the solemn tower of the Guzman, is the convent church of the Dominican Mothers, exactly on the site where the Saint would come into the world. Further west, **Gumiel de Izán** deserves its place on this route, with the splendid high altarpiece from the 15th century by an unknown artist, which can be admired in the parochial church. In the neighboring **La Aguilera**, in the Franciscan convent Domus Dei, the remains of San Pedro Regalado are venerated. The chapel, in which the reliquaries of this Vallodolid saint are kept, possesses interesting altarpieces and various objects that belonged to Isabel the Catholic.

Only 4 km away, **Gumiel del Mercado** is another locality with medieval spirit. Its most noteworthy monument is the fortress-type church of San Pedro, from the 15th century. It also possesses various traditional wine cellars that remind us that we are in the land of wine.

The nearby **Sotillo de la Ribera** also has various wine cellars. Sotillo is a country home with notable buildings worth mentioning, like the Town Hall, the Casa de la Botica (Pharmaceutical House) and the Casa Grande (Big House), from the 17th and 18th cen-

Sotillo de la Ribera: Town Hall and the Casa Grande (Big House).

Roa: bridge over the river Duero.

turies, as well as the church of Santa Águeda, which holds a moving Christ kneeling over the globe of the world and a magnificent marble Christ child, work of sculptor Michelangelo Naccherino.

11 km from Sotillo, **Roa** rises from a spur in the fertile valley of the Duero. Its extensive book of history tells us that here the Romans made the road that unites Clunia with the Leon town of Astorga, or that the cardinal Cisneros died here, in 1517, and Juan Martín "The Stubborn", hero of the War of Independence, was executed in the Plaza Mayor in 1825. Of its artistic heritage, the Collegiate church of Santa María, monumental work from the second third of the 16th century, stands out. Inside, with three large naves, the sculptural group of the adoration of the Three Kings, by Diego de Siloé, is kept. The Gothic choir stalls at the head of the temple should also be mentioned. In Roa, there is the central office of the Regulatory Council for the Denomination of Origin of wine from the Ribera del Duero.

Roa: Collegiate church of Santa María.

Coming from Aranda, **Haza** sits upon a mountain, evoking by means of its castle and wall ruins, the key role it played in the Castillian repopulating of the region.

GASTRONOMY

With simple recipes and first quality products, the Burgos cuisine hasn't only made a name for itself in the rich and varied Spanish gastronomic panorama, but it also makes up one of the principal attractions of this pretty province. Its dish par excellence is the grilled suckling lamb, which is elaborated on low heat in the oven or in a clay casserole. The grilled lamb chops don't get left behind, just like the very famous blood sausage, which is said, not without reason, to be the authentic ambassador of Burgos.

Being a strong, nutritious cuisine, there aren't dishes lacking like the olla podrida, which is prepared with beans, chorizo, bacon, pork ribs and blood sausage. As far as fish, the rivers Arlanza, Arlanzón, Pedroso, Oca and Nela take responsibility for proportioning abundant trout, another basic element of Burgos cuisine. Prepared with ham, in white wine or "a la molinera", it always boast of its exquisite flavor. Less numerous than in the past, river crab have their place on this superficial list of dishes. Typical desserts are cheeses, whether they are white and soft, dry or goat, the almonds of Briviesca, the yolks of Burgos or the pastries of Sobadillo.

For appropriately watering down these succulent morsels, there's nothing better than one of those wines elaborated with the guarantee of quality by the Denomination of Ribera del Duero Origin.

FESTIVALS AND TRADITIONS

Burgos is a land of ancestral and varied traditions that, generation after generation, has been kept alive in the heart of its people. Some of these festivals evoke the presence of Arabs, like those that take place in Peñaranda de Duero, where on September 8, the dance called "Sing la mora" is performed. Others have a more festive character, like those of Briviesca, when at the end of the pilgrimage to the sanctuary of Santa Casilda, the participants pass the time trying to win at the popular game "tabas". But the majority has a religious origin. The processions of Holy Week should be mentioned, especially those on Friday due to their great solemnity, the procession of the Curpillos, the day after Corpus; or the colorful pilgrimage of San Juan del Monte, in

Dishes of Burgos cuisine.

Festivals of San Pedro and San Pablo.

Miranda de Ebro, in which various groups sing and dance while on their way to the shrine of the saint.

Other deep rooted festivals in the province are the dance of the Rueda Chospona, in Covarrubias, with the participation of the whole town, the descent of the Angel, in Aranda de Duero; or the warrior dance of pagan ritual in Espinosa de los Monteros. Burgos, the capital, celebrates its patron saint festivals on June 29 in honor of San Pedro and San Pablo.

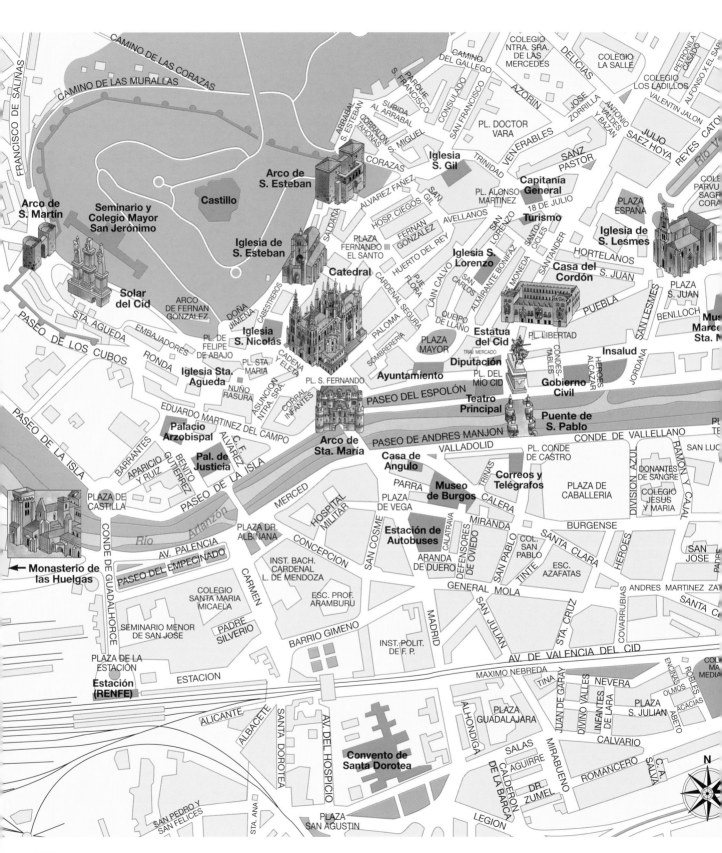

CAMINO DE LAS CORAZAS

CAMINO DE LAS MURALLAS

FRANCISCO DE SALINAS

COLEGIO NTRA. SRA. DE LAS MERCEDES

DELICIAS

COLEGIO LA SALLE

PETRONILA CASADO

COLEGIO LOS LADILLOS

ALFONSO X EL SAB

CAMINO DEL GALLEGO

CONSULADO

AZORIN

JOSE ZORRILLA

VALENTIN JALON

ANTONIO VALDES Y BAZAN

REYES CATO

Río Y

ARRABAL S. ESTEBAN

S. FRANCISCO

PARQUE S. FRANCISCO

SAN FRANCISCO

PL. DOCTOR VARA

JULIO SAEZ HOYA

COLE PARVU SAGR CORA

Arco de S. Esteban

CORRALON S. MIGUEL

SUBIDA AL ARRABAL

TAHONAS

CORAZAS

Iglesia S. Gil

TRINIDAD

VENERABLES

SANZ PASTOR

Capitanía General

PLAZA ESPAÑA

Castillo

ALVAREZ FAÑEZ

PL. ALONSO MARTINEZ

18 DE JULIO

Iglesia de S. Lesmes

Arco de S. Martín

Seminario y Colegio Mayor San Jerónimo

Iglesia de S. Esteban

HOSP. CIEGOS

SALDAÑA

PLAZA FERNANDO III EL SANTO

FERNAN GONZALEZ

AVELLANOS

SAN LORENZO

SANTO CICLES

Turismo

SANTANDER

HORTELANOS

S. JUAN

Catedral

HUERTO DEL REY

Iglesia S. Lorenzo

SAN CARLOS

ALMIRANTE BONIFAZ

MONEDA

Casa del Cordón

PLAZA S. JUAN

SAN LESMES

Mus Marce Sta. M

Solar del Cid

ARCO DE FERNAN GONZALEZ

DOÑA JIMENA

CABESTREROS

Iglesia S. Nicolás

CARDENAL SEGURA

LAIN CALVO

QUEIPO DE LLANO

PALOMA

Estatua del Cid

PL. LIBERTAD

PUEBLA

BENLLOCH

CONDES-TABLES

Insalud

PASEO DE STA. AGUEDA

EMBAJADORES

PL. DE FELIPE DE ABAJO

PJE. FLORA

PLAZA MAYOR

TRAV. MERCADO

Diputación

HEROES ALCAZAR

JORDANA

PASEO DE LOS CUBOS

RONDA

PL. STA. MARIA

CADENA Y ELETA

ASUNCION NTRA. SRA.

PL. S. FERNANDO

SOMBRERERIA

PL. DEL MIO CID

Ayuntamiento

Gobierno Civil

Iglesia Sta. Agueda

NUÑO RASURA

CORRAL INFANTES

PASEO DEL ESPOLÓN

Teatro Principal

EDUARDO MARTINEZ DEL CAMPO

Palacio Arzobispal

C. F. ALVAREZ

Arco de Sta. María

Puente de S. Pablo

CONDE DE VALLELLANO

PL. TE

PASEO DE LA ISLA

BARRANTES

APARICIO Y RUIZ

BENITO GUTIERREZ

Pal. de Justicia

PASEO DE LA ISLA

PASEO DE ANDRES MANJON

Casa de Angulo

VALLADOLID

PL. CONDE DE CASTRO

SAN LUC

RAMON Y CAJAL

DIVISION AZUL

DONANTES DE SANGRE

PLAZA DE CASTILLA

CONDE DE GUADALHORCE

Río Arlanzón

PLAZA DR. ALBIÑANA

MERCED

PARRA

PLAZA DE VEGA

Museo de Burgos

Correos y Telégrafos

CALERA

PLAZA DE CABALLERIA

COLEGIO JESUS Y MARIA

← Monasterio de las Huelgas

AV. PALENCIA

PASEO DEL EMPECINADO

CONCEPCION

HOSPITAL MILITAR

SAN COSME

Estación de Autobuses

CALATRAVA

MIRANDA

DEFENSORES DE OVIEDO

SAN PABLO

COL. SAN PABLO

SANTA CLARA

BURGENSE

HEROES

SAN JOSE

PADRE

INST. BACH. CARDENAL L. DE MENDOZA

CARMEN

ARANDA DE DUERO

TINTE

ESC. AZAFATAS

ANDRES MARTINEZ ZAT

SANTA C

COLEGIO SANTA MARIA MICAELA

ESC. PROF. ARAMBURU

GENERAL MOLA

SAN JULIAN

STA. CRUZ

COVARRUBIAS

SEMINARIO MENOR DE SAN JOSE

PADRE SILVERIO

BARRIO GIMENO

INST. POLIT. DE F. P.

MADRID

AV. DE VALENCIA DEL CID

PLAZA DE LA ESTACIÓN

ESTACION

MAXIMO NEBREDA

TINA

JUAN DE GARAY

DIVINO VALLES

INFANTES DE LARA

NEVERA

ENCINAS

OLMOS

ROBLES

COL MA MEDIA

Estación (RENFE)

ALICANTE

ALBACETE

SANTA DOROTEA

AV. DEL HOSPICIO

ALHONDIGA

PLAZA GUADALAJARA

SALAS

AGUIRRE

CALDERON DE LA BARCA

MIRABUENO

PLAZA S. JULIAN

ACACIAS

ABETO

CALVARIO

ROMANCERO

C. A. SALVA

Convento de Santa Dorotea

DR. ZUMEL

LEGION

N

SAN PEDRO Y SAN FELICES

STA. ANA

PLAZA SAN AGUSTIN

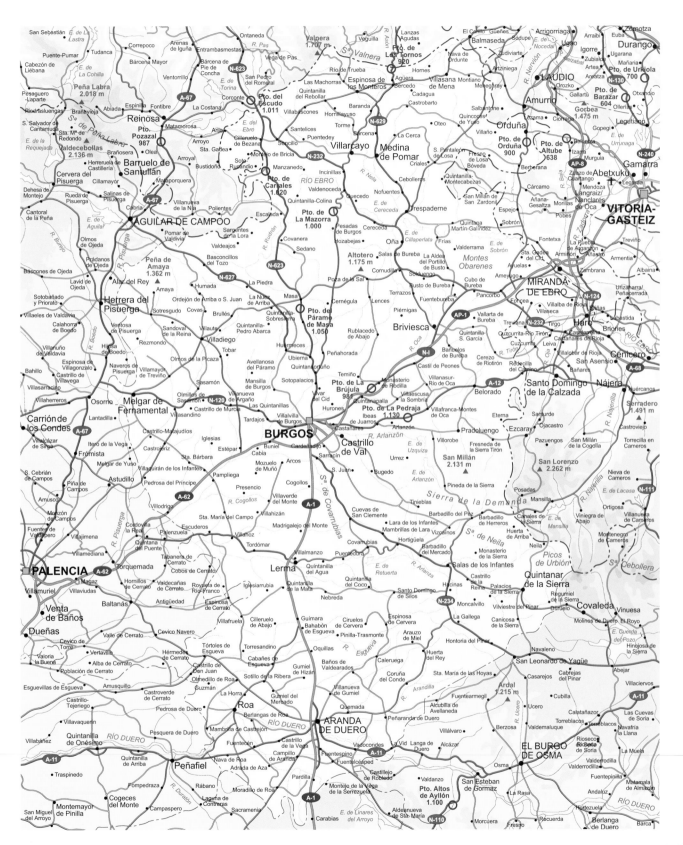

CONTENTS

EDITORIAL FISA ESCUDO DE ORO, S.A.
Tel: 93 230 86 00
www.eoro.com

I.S.B.N. 978-84-378-2509-0
Printed in Spain
Legal Dep. B. 10749-2008